MW01280392

MISSISSIPPI MIRTH

This book is dedicated to my loving wife Brenda and grandchildren August, Kamran and Stella

Front and back cover photograph by Erik Berg
Cover design by Erik Berg

ISBN: 978-0-9778339-1-7

ACKNOWLEDGEMENTS

I would to thank everyone who lent a hand in getting this project off the ground. First of all, I could not have done a thing without the generous love and support of my wife Brenda. The same goes for my extended family: Shanon Benson, Fawn Witt, and Conor McCaffrey along with our grandchildren August, Kamran, and Stella. Next, I want to thank my two editors I fortunately have had the opportunity to work with over the past six years, Julie Berg Raymond with Tapestry Magazine and Aryn Nichols with Inspire(d) Magazine. You both have provided wonderful insight and guidance to me for the Mississippi Mirth columns project. I also need to thank Tanya O'Connor, co-owner of Tapestry Magazine and Benji Nichols, co-owner of Inspire(d) Magazine for all of your support. That brings us to the other two big contributors to the cause, Deb Paulson with layout and Erik Berg with cover pictures and cover design. You guys are just wonderful to work with.

Also my greatest thanks to the staff at Dolce Vita. Your ability to cover for me to make this book happen made it happen. There is a whole slew of people also who had their pictures in these columns and I would like to thank them as well. A special thanks goes out to all of the following for their last minute help getting pictures to us, Karla Presler for her picture of her late husband, Art; Barry Levenson for his Mustard Museum Curator portrait, Arnoldo and Angel Barrientos for "Chile and the Man" photos, and Gail Bolson for her Festival of Trees photo.

If I have left anyone out it surely was not intended and my apologies are given.

TAPESTRY MAGAZINE COLUMNS
2007 - 2009

INTRODUCTION
TAPESTRY MAGAZINE

Since my Mississippi Mirth column got its start with Tapestry Magazine, I thought it would be appropriate to begin with the magazine's review of my book, "Midwest Cornfusion." Julie Berg Raymond, Arts and Lifestyle editor for the Decorah Newspapers, wrote that article for the December 7, 2006, issue of the Decorah Journal. With permission, she reprinted the piece in January 2007 for Tapestry Magazine Julie was co-owner, with Tanya OConnor, and editor of that magazine, which was distributed up and down the Mississippi River Valley form Minneapolis/St Paul to St Louis. It was a great read and I looked forward to it every month.

So, I decided to throw my hat in the ring and cajole Julie and Tanya to let me write a humorous food column for Tapestry. Julie replied "That would be great, except we already have a great food writer." I remarked, "Julie, Tanya, Details! Details! Why don't we think outside the box? What other magazine in the Midwest has two food writers?" "OK, OK," Julie came back. "I'll call Jeff Severson (Tapestry food writer extraordinaire) and see how he feels about it." Turns out that Jeff loved the idea and embraced it enthusiastically. Julie told me later what sold them on the idea is that it would be a humorous column. Jeff and I had a lot of fun with our columns throwing out the occasional zing at one other. Great camaraderie. When we opened up McCaffrey's Dolce Vita and Twin Springs Bakery, Jeff came down with his lovely wife, Lisa, and wrote a review of the restaurant for Tapestry. I thought it would be appropriate to finish off our Tapestry section with it. It is reprinted from the November 2008 issue of Tapestry magazine.

This is provided with permission of Julie, Tanya and Jeff. Thanks to the Decorah Newspapers and Tapestry magazine for all of your support.

MIDWEST CORN FUSION:
A COLLECTION OF RECIPES AND HUMOR

by James McCaffrey. 2006. (200 pp. $18.95)

Reviewed by Julie Berg-Raymond

Tapestry Magazine January 2007

This article first appeared in the Decorah Journal, Dec. 7, 2006 and is reprinted here courtesy of the Decorah Newspapers.

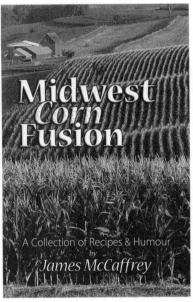

People who know Jim McCaffrey know that he likes his food on the spicy side.

People who know Northeast Iowa know that this has tended to leave McCaffrey in a bit of a quandry, through the years.

In the spirit of good humor and inventiveness that has long characterized the rural Decorah, Iowa resident -- one-time owner of the former (and famous) Cafe Deluxe, and McCaffreys' Supper Club -- McCaffrey has had some fun with the fact that his own tastebuds and the culinary culture of his home region haven't always been in synch.

"This chapter contains recipes that I have created and/or shared over the years with my Norwegian friends that have a little kick to them," McCaffrey writes in the first chapter of his recently-published cookbook, Midwest Corn Fusion: A Collection of Recipes and Humor. *"Most have said, 'mange tak' (many thanks). Others have just ran down the street yelling obscenities about an Irish cook who has just challenged their taste buds..."*

And so begins the humorous, big-hearted, deliciously inspiring ode to the food of the Upper Midwest that is *Midwest Corn Fusion*.

The cookbook was over a year in development, McCaffrey says, although the recipes it contains have come together over many years of loving to cook. He enjoys preparing intimate dinners for friends and family as much as he does making food in larger amounts -- helping cook up two thousand hot dogs, say, in four hours, as he did at the Mustard Museum's National Mustard Days in Mt. Horeb, WI last summer. As a result, Midwest Corn Fusion offers recipes suitable for both small family meals (his homemade Macaroni and Cheese comes enticingly to mind) and bigger feeds -- McCaffrey's own "Cafe Deluxe Chili" recipe is here, and can be expanded upon as the crowd dictates.

A word about that mustard museum. McCaffrey devotes a chapter to mustard-inspired recipes ("The Mighty Yellow Condiment, or Do You Know the Mustard Man?"); there, he introduces his friend and condiment-loving cohort, Barry Levenson, curator of the museum that opened in 1986 and currently houses well over 4,400 different mustards from all over the world. For more information about the museum and about the National Mustard Days held each August, visit www.mustardweb.com.

The Mustard Man isn't the only notable Midwestern "foodie" we meet in the cookbook. In "BBQ Chapter: Big Daddy lives in our hearts forever," McCaffrey pays tribute to the late "Ike" Issac Seymour, better known as "Big Daddy," formerly of Des Moines. Legendary in Iowa for his barbeque and homemade sauces, writes McCaffrey, "his generosity is what always made him my hero. He donated thousands of dollars to the Iowa Food Bank, helped needy elementary schoolchildren with clothes and meals, had Thanksgiving turkeys on the tables of the less fortunate, and the list goes on and on."

The barbeque chapter, alone -- with more on the story of Big Daddy, and recipes for everything from Kansas City-style baby back ribs to blackened salmon to Prosciutto-wrapped shrimp -- will probably be considered worth the book's cover price; but a perusal of the rib-tickling, mouth-watering Table of Contents should seal the deal for anyone interested in the real variety and diversity to be found in the cuisine of the Upper Midwest.

From chapters on "Spicing Up Norway" and "Flim Flamming at the Farmers Market," to "Grin and Beer It" and "What Goes on the Cornfield Stays in the Cornfield!," Jim McCaffrey's cookbook entertains, inspires, and nourishes -- which is exactly what a good cookbook should do.

Midwest Corn Fusion is available in Decorah, IA at Agora Arts, Ace Kitchen Place, Bookends and Beans, Oneota Community Co-op, and Your Place and at independent booksellers throughout the tri-state region.

HOMEMADE MAC & CHEESE

The kids will never want that stuff from the blue box again. Try this out and have the kids give you a hand. I like to start with the basic recipe and just add whatever I like for that day (i.e., chopped onions, green or red peppers, mushrooms, etc.).

2 cups elbow macaroni, cooked to
   package directions and drained

1 tbl. olive oil

2 1/2 cups milk

2 tbl. cornstarch

1/2 stick butter

1/2 small onion, grated

1/2 tsp. dry mustard

1/4 tsp. worcester sauce

Salt and pepper to taste

6 oz. cheddar cheese, shredded

1/4 cup crushed saltine crackers or
   Italian breadcrumbs

Fresh parsley (optional)

Grease a two-quart casserole dish with olive oil or butter. Put cooked macaroni in casserole and toss with 1 tbl. olive oil. Stir cornstarch into milk in a medium saucepan. Add butter, onion, mustard, worcester sauce, and salt/pepper to taste. Over medium heat stir constantly and bring to a boil. Lower heat and gradually add cheese. Continue to stir for about two minutes or until cheese melts. Mix with macaroni and sprinkle on crackers or breadcrumbs. Bake in preheated oven at 350 degrees until cheese is bubbly, about 10 minutes. Garnish individual servings with sprigs of fresh parsley.

TAPESTRY MAGAZINE 2007

VALENTINE'S DAY

Tapestry Magazine Feburary 2007

It's February and time to put some effort into Valentine's Day. What to do?

Well, instead of wondering "what can I do for my Valentine?," how about asking "what can we do together?" Specifically, how about working together on a beautiful dinner for the two of you?

(When I asked Brenda, my wife and best friend of the last 27 years, if she liked my idea she said "Great! I can pour the wine.")

Have a wonderful Valentine's Day and enjoy life with your sweetheart.

DEVILS ON HORSEBACK (PROSCIUTTO WRAPPED SHRIMP)

6 large shrimp (15-20 count)

3 strips thin sliced prosciutto, halved (or thin sliced bacon)

1/2 cup mayonaise

3 Tbl. chili sauce

1 Tbl. finely diced dill pickles

1 Tbl. finely diced onion

1-2 tsp. coarse ground brown mustard

Salt and freshly ground black pepper

Wrap each shrimp with a half slice of prosciutto. Pin with a tooth pick. Combine remaining ingredients and chill. When ready to serve, fire up the bbq grille. Over medium to medium high heat and a very clean grill surface, grill shrimp. Turn often until shrimp turns pink, 2-3 minutes. Serve immediately with chilled sauce.

HAIL TO CAESAR SALAD WITH GORGANZOLA

1 peeled garlic clove

2 Tbl fresh lemon juice

3/4 Tsp salt

1 Tbl red wine vinegar

1/4 Tsp fresh ground black pepper

1 Tsp Worcestershire sauce

1 Tbl Dijon style mustard

6 anchovy fillets, chopped

1 large fresh egg

1 head romaine lettuce

1/4 cup extra virgin olive oil

1/4 loaf rustic French bread

2 oz. Gorgonzola or Bleu Cheese

In a large serving bowl, add salt and pepper. Mash garlic clove in salt and wipe around bowl. Stir mustard in. Whisk egg into mixture. Stir in olive oil. Slowly stir in lemon and red wine vinegar. Add Worcestershire sauce and anchovies and mix. Wash lettuce and cut off stem. Chop into large bite sized pieces and toss with dressing. Cube bread into 3/8 inch cubes. Heat about 2 tbl olive oil in a large skillet to med/med-high heat. Add bread cubes and saute until golden (about 3-4 minutes). Drain on paper towels and salt pepper to taste. Garnish salad with bread cubes and gorgonzola.

Note: If you have concerns of using raw egg because of salmonella risk, use a pasteurized or coddled egg. To coddle, add1egg to boiling water for exactly 1 minute. Take out, break shell, and whisk.

CAPPELINI WITH BAY SCALLOPS

Extra virgin olive oil

Salt

4-5 large fresh tomatoes, diced

Fresh ground black pepper

1 lb uncooked bay scallops

1/2 medium red onion, diced

2 cloves garlic, minced

6 oz angel hair pasta

1/4 cup unpacked fresh basil leaves

Start pasta water immediately. In a large skillet, saute tomatoes, onions, and garlic 3-4 minutes in 1-2 tbl olive oil. Add basil and saute 30 seconds more. Salt and pepper to taste. If using scallops, cappellini sauce is ready when scallops turn white. At the same time, cook noodles according to package directions and drain. Serve sauce over top of noodles immediately for best results. This truly is a dish where some good rustic garlic bread is great to mop up any remaining sauce on one's plate.

GARLIC BREAD

1/3 loaf rustic French bread

6 tbl extra virgin olive oil

1 garlic clove, minced

Preheat oven to 375. Cut bread in two the long way. In a small sauce pan heat oil and garlic over medium heat 2-3 minutes.

Brush on bread and heat in oven until toasty, 8-10 minutes.

(You can always put some grated parmesan or asiago cheese as well, just before inserting bread in oven).

CHOCOLATE DIPPED STRAWBERRIES

12 Fresh strawberries with stem, rinsed and completely dried

5 oz. Dark baking chocolate

In a double boiler set up, bring 1 inch of water to boil.

Set second pot over. Add chocolate and melt. Stir until smooth. Roll strawberries in chocolate and place on a sheet of wax paper on a cookie sheet. Refridgerate for at least 1/2 hour.

MUSTARD JUDGE

Tapestry Magazine March 2007

This is my account of three days in the life of a mustard judge.

The 2007 Napa Valley Worldwide Mustard Competition was held in Mt. Horeb, WI on two consecutive Sundays, Jan. 27 and Feb. 4, 2007. The 18 category champions were taste-tested for an overall grand champion, "Best of Show," on Feb. 18.

I embark in my trusty steed, a 1991 Ford Aerostar --166,000+ miles; red, with a complete rustline around the bottom; white front-quarter panel (thank you, Mr. Deer); slipping transmission; and virtually no heat. Other than that, she's cherry!

I arrive in Mt. Horeb and proceed to the Mustard Museum, host of this prestigious event. Barry Levenson, curator of the Museum's 4,600-plus jars of different mustards from throughout the world, and his wonderful wife, Patti (Mrs. Mustard), greet all of the judges effusively. There are thirty-five judges, total. Thirty-four are of impeccable stature and one is a shanty-Irish cook (that's me). There are 370 different mustards, entered into 18 categories.

I am seated at a table of nine; we will be judging three types of mustard today -- all mustards entered are from commercial enterprises only. The first category is "Sweet Hot," with 33 entries. On a scale of 1 to 10 we judge each for quality (does it meet the category?), and how well we like it (the "yummy factor"). Thirty-three passes and an hour later, our palates have graduated summa cum laude from the prestigious college of Poupon U.

We move on to "Spirit Mustard" (22 alcohol-infused mustards). Our last category, "Exotic Mustards," includes a nut-based mustard and a chocolate mustard.

Eighty three mustards later, I'm on my way home, a better mustard man.

The next Sunday, yellow fever hits. I judge the finalists in seven other categories. There are a total of 75 golden concoctions that most certainly challenge my taste buds. WOW! -- get this: deli, honey, herb, fruit, Dijon, organic and classic hot ... Talk about a marathon menagerie of mustard!

Two Sundays later, we are blind taste-testing again. This time we are choosing the grand champion of all of the 18 finalists, "Best of Show." It is extremely difficult.

We rate each mustard from 1 to 18. Each mustard must have a number assigned to it or the ballot is disqualified. There are eighteen wonderful finalists, each tremendous in its own right. I begin by tasting each mustard and make a few notes on each. Then I start working backward, eliminating one by one, re-tasting and re-tasting all along. Fourteen mighty mustards are commiserating about not being chosen, and I hit a wall. I honestly like each of the remaining mustards. I think they can each be "Best of Show." They are Sweet Hot, Deli Brown, Fruit, and Coarse-Grained. My final choice is Deli Brown.

Tune in next month for the exciting results of "The Best of the Golden Condiment Quest."

COLONEL MUSTARD IN THE KITCHEN WINGS

4 lbs chicken wings	3 tbl. fresh lime juice
Cajun seasoning	3 tbl. mayonnaise
1 cup Dijon-style mustard	1/2 tsp. salt

Preheat oven to 350 degrees. Wash chicken wings with cold water and remove any remaining feathers. Pat dry. Cut wings apart at joints and either save the small tip ends and freeze to make stock with later or discard. Place wing pieces on a large cookie sheet/ baking pan. Sprinkle with Cajun seasoning. Turn pieces over and sprinkle again. Place in oven for 20 minutes. Pull out and turn pieces over. Place in oven for another 20 minutes or until juices run clear. Mix mustard, lime juice, mayonnaise, and salt together. When wings are cooked, place in a large mixing bowl. Stir in mustard sauce and coat thoroughly. Return to baking sheet and cook an additional 10 minutes. Serve immediately.

BACON AND SPINACH SALAD WITH MUSTARD DRESSING
(Serves 4)

1 lb. fresh spinach, washed
and stemmed
1 tbl. Honey
1 lb. chopped bacon
salt

fresh ground black pepper
1 tbl. Dijon-style mustard
1 small red onion, sliced thin
2 tbl. Red wine vinegar
2-3 hard boiled eggs, sliced

Using a heavy skillet, fry bacon over medium heat until crisp. Remove to paper towels. Save bacon drippings. Whisk mustard, vinegar and honey into drippings to make the dressings. Season with salt and pepper. Toss spinach with dressing and bacon pieces. Serve in a nice salad bowl and top with sliced onions and eggs.

KITCHEN COLLECTOR

Tapestry Magazine April 2007

In Venice, Italy: Ristorante da Bruno. This also leads to a another glass of ambrosia -- and I pop the question: "May I have a peek into your kitchen?"

My wife, Brenda, and I love to travel. And like everyone else, we pick some local souvenirs to share with the family. You know, t-shirts that say "Mom and Dad went to Timbuktu and all I got was this lousy t-shirt" or "My parents are spending my inheritance in South Dakota." Truly treasures of our modern society.

Actually, Brenda has collected some very wonderful pieces over the years: Black clay pottery from Oaxaca, Mexico; glass pieces from Murano, Italy; carnival masks from Venice and a charcoal portrait of Brenda done in the Plaza Navonne in Rome, to mention a few. I , however, happen to dance to the beat of a different life force. I collect the vibrant soul of all these exotic places. In other words, I collect kitchens.

We go to restaurants to experience cuisine sensations new to our taste palates. Sometimes said sensations are accompanied by two or three glasses of properly aged grape ambrosia. This leads to the proper introduction of our wait staff. By this time they'll have decided that we are going to be big tippers and they are going to go to almost any extreme for us. This also leads to a another glass of ambrosia -- and I pop the question: "May I have a peek into your kitchen?"

"Oh, but of course" is the usual answer. They lead me in, introduce the cooks, and Brenda takes pictures. Boy, do we know how to have a good time!

We were in Venice, Italy one time with our good friends, Jack and Sheryl, and went to eat at Ristorante Da Bruno. The usual banter proceeded, and I'm on my way to the kitchen with two waiters. The kitchen staff meets us and we're about to head in the kitchen when the owner stops us and says "No way." The waiters and kitchen staff start to argue with him. In the midst of the argument, a young woman cook grabs my arm and yanks me into the kitchen. A pasta order comes up. She makes the noodles and has me make the sauce. I lay out the plate, garnish it, and set it up to be served. The owner sees this and is grinning from ear to ear. We take pictures of him and he gives us presents to take with us. What a gas! Not bad, considering I don't speak any Italian.

PASTA AND FAGIOLI SOUP

2 Tbl Extra virgin olive oil

4 cups chicken broth

2 cloves garlic, minced

3 15 oz. cans cannellini beans

1/2 red onion, diced

1 15 oz. can diced tomatoes

2 med. Carrots, peeled and diced

10 button mushrooms, sliced

4 slices cooked pancetta or bacon, diced

1/2 cup small macaroni noodles

4 cups water

2 oz. grated parmesan cheese

2 4 oz cans diced green chile

Salt and fresh ground black pepper to taste

In a large pot, saute garlic, onion, and carrots about 4 minutes. Set aside in food processor or blender. Add bacon, water, chile, and broth to the pot. Add one can of beans, tomatoes, and mushrooms. Blend the remaining beans with garlic, onions, and carrots. Toss back into pot. Meanwhile, cook pasta according to package directions. Drain and add to pot. Bring soup to a simmer, add parmesan, salt and pepper. Goes great some rustic bread. Enjoy!!

Note: Winner of the Napa Valley Worldwide Mustard Competition was Sierra Nevada Stout and Stoneground Mustard. Congratulations!

THERE'S FUNGUS AMONGST US

Tapestry Magazine May 2007

"Oz never did give nothin' to the Tin Man that he didn't already have."

Boy, I wish I had come up with that line. In Northeast Iowa, the first three weeks of May could well be a gift from Oz. Morels are popping and shroomers are plucking. A grand and noble sporting event!

I have been hunting morels for most of my teenage and adult life. I have more secret spots to find these delectable delights than a leopard has. In a couple of minutes I am going to share these spots with you.

But first, a few tips on making the mushroom hunt (called shrooming) an enjoyable one. First, it's wood/deertick season -- so wear a hat, a light-colored long sleeve shirt with arms buttoned, long pants and, like your mother told you, wear good shoes.

I always take a walking stick to help on steep slopes and to search under leaves and tall grass for those wily morels. I use a large netted onion bag to carry those little treasures in. This helps spread spores far and wide. I refuse to use plastic bread sacks or garbage bags. I find this approach tends to break down the mushrooms at a much faster rate. A paper grocery bag will work in a pinch. And speaking of pinches, that is how to pick morels. Pinch or cut them above ground. If you pull them out of the ground, it cuts the possibility of re-growth next year to zero. That's the theory, anyway.

If you are a novice shroomer in the upper Mississippi valley region, probably the easiest places to find morels are around dead elm trees that have just started to lose their bark. A lot of conditions come into play for mushrooms to pop. The biggest are ground moisture and ground temperature. Tops of south facing slopes are usually first to sprout, east/west, and then north. I haven't been skunked yet, but sometimes getting your eyes adjusted to find that first shroom can be a little tough. But, when you do, it's like a present from Oz! And finding a mother lode is like manna from heaven.

Five Biggest Shroomer Lies:

5. They are not out yet.

4. I found them five miles from here.

3. I most certainly do have permission to hunt here.

2. I'm just out here picking spring flowers.

1. Sure, I'll share my secret hunting spots with you!

I will, however, share a favorite morel mushroom recipe with you.

MOREL AND GREEN CHILE SOUP

When we had McCaffrey's Supper Club we always had two or three soups on. This is a version of our signature soup, adapted from my book, Midwest Cornfusion.

(12-16 servings)

Morel Broth

2 qts. chicken broth

2 qts water

1 lb. fresh morels

1 can diced green chiles

1 small red onion, diced

3 cloves garlic, minced

Salt and fresh ground black pepper to taste

Roux

2 1/4 sticks butter

2 cups flour

Combine all Morel Broth ingredients in a large pot and bring to a boil for 3 minutes. Reduce to a simmer. Melt butter in a 2-3 gallon heavy bottom pot over low heat. Add flour and stir constantly for 12 minutes, pulling off heat occasionally. Do not let burn. If you see black flecks you will have to start over. Turn off heat. This is your Roux. Pour broth into roux pot and stir. Cook over medium heat until soup thickens (1-3 minutes). Get ready for OZ.

HEY, WHO CUT THE CHEESE?

Tapestry Magazine June 2007

June is Dairy Month.

Which means that in Wisconsin, Northeast Iowa, and Southeast Minneasota there is a thirty-day moratorium on cow tipping.

So while my fellow columnist, Jeff Severson, and his lovely wife, Lisa, were out touring the beautiful hills and valleys of the Mississippi river searching for that perfect glass of wine, I have have been painstakingly pursuing the perfect accompaniment, cheese.

I decided to use a scientific approach and use the ancient art of elimination. First to go was processed American Cheese. Candlelight, soft music, a bottle of vintage 1998 cabernet sauvignon, and and a couple slices of plastic-wrapped aged milk just didn't seem to cut it.

Next to go was stinky cheese. Limburger lovers are probably going to put an evil hex on me, but I think this type of cheese will fare better with a cold glass of pale ale.

Obviously, Cottage Cheese isn't going to make "A" list. Well, maybe with some Boone's farm. No, let's not go there. Same with ricotta.

Maybe we need to go to a foreign country.

Remember the movie, "French Kiss"? The scene where Meg Ryan, on the train, explains to Kevin Kline that there are over 400 varieties of cheesee in France? They make some great wines as well. My only problem with that avenue is I'm not very familiar with French cheeses.

Since my wife, Brenda, son Conor, and I are going to Southern France in September, I may be able to address that issue later.

But don't despair, Jeff and Lisa. There is a foreign country that I am familiar with and that is Italy. Many great cheeses and many great wines.

Today's cheese is going into a wonderful dish called risotto. If you haven't had it you have to try it. And if you have had it, you know exactly what I'm talking about. The aforementioned cheese salutes from the town of Parma along with town's other famous food, Prosciutto. By now you've probably deduced that we are talking Parmesan.

Parmesan is a hard, nutty cheese that is very salty and very delicious. So when you buy it, always buy it in the block form, not shredded. It tends to lose its zing.

Try it in this risotto recipe. Add your favorite white wine -- and leave cow tipping to the frat boys.

BASIC RISOTTO

1/2 small onion, diced fine

2 cloves garlic, minced

3 tbl extra virgin olive oil

1 1/2 cups arborio rice

1/2 cup dry white wine

5 cups chicken broth heated to a boil

1 cup fresh grated Parmesan Cheese

1 cup fresh or frozen peas

1/4 cup butter

Salt and Fresh ground black pepper to taste

Saute onion and garlic in olive oil on medium heat until soft, about 3 minutes. Add rice and saute until translucent, about 5 minutes. Warm the wine on the stove. Add to the rice and stir untl it is absorbed. Add broth a ladle at a time and let it absorb as well. Keep stirring. When rice is tender, shut off heat. Add butter, 1/2 of the cheese and peas. Mix gently. Season with salt and pepper. Serve and pass the remaining cheese around.

Chef's note: Arborio rice can be found in larger grocery stores. It is stocked in the Oneota Community Co-op in Decorah, IA. Happy Eating

BE WILLING, BE CHILLING, BE GRILLING

Tapestry Magazine July 2007

"Summer time, and the livin' is easy..."

Time to be spending time outside communing with nature. My semi-beautiful wife, Brenda, and I have started hiking to get into marvelous, simply marvelous, shape. It's amazing how out of shape a person can get in a mere 55 years. Actually, eight years ago we hiked from the south rim of the Grand Canyon -- down and up 17 miles, in one day. So we have been in somewhat reasonable shape -- at least, eight years ago we were.

We are fortunate to live next to Twin Springs Park in Decorah, IA. We can just walk from our house and hike in Twin Springs Park or further down the road in Phelps Park. A couple of weeks ago, after completing a great hike, I was almost

back to our house when two great horned owls began hooting back and forth to each other. It was just incredible to realize these magnificent creatures were nesting in the woods right by our own nest, so to speak.

I started thinking about how lucky we all are for the wonderful park systems around Decorah -- and all over the upper Mississippi Valley. I also thought about how seldom we might utilize these great resources. When is the last time you went on a picnic and enjoyed the great outdoors?

With those thoughts in mind, I decided to devote this month's column to one of my favorite outside activities... playing with fire. Ever since the earliest times, man has had a fascination with fire. Pictures come to mind: Emperor Nero playing the violin while Rome burnt around him; the Vikings sending their dearly beloved out to sea in burning burial boats (that would be the Scandinavians, not the Minnesota football team); and a memory comes to mind from my childhood when we were out cutting wood for the farmhouse. We would make enormous piles of the left-over limbs and brush and, in winter, my dad would douse the brush pile with enough gasoline to drive to Rockford and back. Then he would back up, retrieve his trusty double 16-gauge shotgun, and let fly with both barrels of #4 shot -- and a raging mountain of fire ensued. More fun than a night with the carnies at the county fair.

My playing with fire these days revolves mostly around food on the BBQ grill. Pretty tame compared to shotgun-inspired infernos. Here are a couple of recipes to share with friends and family. Remember the BBQ golden rules:

1. BE WILLING to be the person in charge and make it happen.

2. BE CHILLING with a cold one, and make sure everyone else is as well.

3. BE GRILLING (Need I say more?).

Stay tuned next for my report -- "MAN OVERBOARD" -- on 10 supposedly sane adults cruising the Mississippi for three days. Sounds like big trouble in river city.

And, remember: Wealth is what you have when the money runs out.

BBQ CHICKEN

2 cut up chicken fryers

6 oz. your favorite BBQ sauce

Original Mrs. Dash

6 oz. medium picante sauce

3 cloves garlic, minced

Juice of 1 large lemon

Preheat oven to 325 degrees. Place chicken in single layers in couple baking pans. Sprinkle chicken with Mrs. Dash. Bake 20 minutes. Turn chicken over and sprinkle the other sides with Mrs. Dash. Bake another 20-30 minutes until juices run clear when pierced with a knife. In meantime fire up the grill and make sure the grates are clean. Combine garlic, BBQ sauce, picante sauce, and lemon juice. Remove chicken to a clean platter. Place on grill and brown one side. Turn over and baste browned side with sauce. Repeat again.

Take off grill and place in large bowl. Cover with any remaining sauce and let the party begin.

GRILLED SWEET CORN

1 dozen ears fresh sweet corn

1/4 lb. butter

1 fresh lime

1/4 - 1/2 tsp. cayenne pepper

Fire up BBQ grill to medium heat. Husk the corn while grill is warming up.

Break off stem and try to pick off as many tassel strands as possible. Melt butter in a small sauce pan. Add about a tablespoon of fresh lime juice and the cayenne pepper. Stir and remove from heat. Place ears of corn on the grill. Keep turning until ears are browned on all sides. Take off grill and pass around the lime pepper butter. OH MY!

MAN OVERBOARD, PART 1
(A CLOSED MIND IS A WONDERFUL THING TO LOSE...)

Tapestry Magazine August 2007

The names in the following story have been changed to protect the guilty.

On Friday, June 8, 2007, the Decorah Wildlife Association -- consisting of Captain Lucky, his lovely wife and first mate, Happy Go and eight unruly boatswains -- embarked from Port McGregor, Iowa.

Aye, Captain -- surely t'was a sight for sore eyes to behold. Captain Lucky steered the lumbering vessel into the main channel with his first mate,

Happy Go, at his side to alert him of interesting scenery, wildlife -- and, lest I forget, impending disasters. The eight unruly boatswains scurried forward and aft, partaking in meaningful duties like filling tankards with libations of various ilk.

Introductions are in order, of course. There was Diamond Dave with his pegleg wife (henceforth to be referred to as Spark). Doc Holiday and his lovely bride, Nurse Why-Not-Chirp, were in attendance, as well. The Lion King and his childhood sweetheart, "J" the River Queen, were on board and enjoying the view with Father Mac, the defrocked Irish priest, and Sister not-abstaining-anymore Bre.

Hands ever steady, Captain Lucky maneuvered the water hotel up the main channel past the overhead bridge, Gilligan's Island, and other points of interest. First on the itinerary was a scheduled visit to the magnanimous Lord and Lady of the river, Mr. and Mrs. McCouple. The McCouples had invited Captain Lucky, Happy Go and the eight unruly boatswains to stop and refresh themselves with some adult beverages.

Did I mention impending disaster?

At that very moment, Captain Lucky was heading into the McCouples' boat landing with Happy Go and the 8 unruly boatswains all shouting directions. "Left!"; "Right!"; "Faster!"; "Full speed ahead!" and such. Needless to say, Captain Lucky was not able to react to all directions at the same time. At least the McCouples' and their neighbors' docks ended up being still functional.

Deciding that perhaps this was not the best docking place for a boat of its size, the group headed over to Baileys Island while Mr. McCouple called his insurance team. The Captain and Mr. McCouple had set up a tent on the island to reserve a space for the boat on the previous day. Upon arriving, the tent was found to be missing along with the Bailey's Island sign.

Such hooliganism! The rest of the day was spent frolicking in the water, sunbathing, engaging in enlightening conversations, and cooking massive New York Strip steaks with aluminum foiled potatoes and marvelous salad. Copious drinking was found to be mandatory, especially for the Irish contingent -- which, by the end of the evening, everyone professed to be.

Stay tuned for next month's conclusion of the saga of Captain Lucky and Happy Go and the eight unruly boatswains. Find out what Diamond Dave and Sparky's little secret is, what The Lion King and "J" the River Queen have to say about sleeping under the stars, what Nurse-Why-Not-Chirp whispered into Doc Holiday's ear, and whether Father Mac and Sister Bre will change their ways...

ALUMINUM FOILED POTATOES

5 lbs new red potatoes, scrubbed and diced

1 large red onion, diced

8 oz. fresh button mushrooms, sliced

2 red bell peppers, destemmed, deseeded, and diced

2 medium carrots, peeled and diced

4 cloves garlic, minced

1/2 lb butter, cut into small pieces

Salt and fresh ground black pepper to taste

Combine all ingredients on a large sheet of heavy duty aluminum foil. Foil needs to be large enough to cover on top and bottom. Make sure to evenly distribute all ingredients. Crimp foil edges together. Turn over and repeat with more foil. Turn again and repeat once more. The idea is to prevent butter from leaking out. Cook over medium high heat, turning frequently. I sometimes use a baking sheet on top and on bottom to help turn the potato mixture without ripping the foil.

PERFECT NEW YORK STRIP OR RIBEYE STEAKS

2 8-10 oz. steaks 1 inch thick

Have steaks at room temperature. Grill over medium high heat for 4 minutes or until juices appear on top side. Flip and grill for 1 more minute for medium rare.

MAN OVERBOARD, PART 2
(A CLOSED MIND IS A WONDERFUL THING TO LOSE...)

Tapestry Magazine September 2007

When we last left Captain Lucky, First Mate Happy Go, and the eight unruly boatswains, they were all headed to bunk for a group snore and dreams of things to come.

During the night, J, the River Queen, rose to the call of nature and proceeded to the head. But a slight misstep (hey, it was dark) propelled her through the night into the sleepspace of Doc Holiday and Nurse Why-Not-Chirp. Arousing from dream state, Nurse Why-Not-Chirp whispered into Doc Holiday's ear, "Do you think we should ask if she would like a cocktail?"

The rest of the night proceeded splendidly. Then, duly refreshed from a great night's sleep, the mates gave a rousing cheer to each other. It was wonderful to be alive and well on the Mighty Mississippi. A gorgeous morning was to be had, complete with a scrumptious breakfast of poultry ovum mixed with fresh garden vegetables, pan-fried potatoes, leftover massive New York strip steaks, mimosas, and fired-up Bloody Marys. It was time to get on with the day's festivities. An excursion to the south of Port McGregor was on the schedule for the day. Captain Lucky, with Happy Go ever present at his side, steered the mammoth vessel into the main channel and headed downriver.

Another visit was in store, this time at the river home of the Pizza King and his lovely wife, the Schoolmarm. A late morning party was in full swing. Captain Lucky maneuvered into the Pizza King's dock with Diamond Dave securing the mooring. The eight unruly boatswains scampered up the bank, followed by Captain Lucky and Happy Go. A good time was had by all. Even the Radio Flyer from Decorah showed up in his bright yellow speed boat. Too soon, it was time to embark and head for Gilligan's Island where a few hundred river denizens were frolicking in the sun on the sand bar.

After an hour of frolicking, the crew headed upstream for the evening's docking. A candlelight evening meal was had, complete with lasagna, salad, garlic bread, fine wine, and excellent conversation. A bonfire was lit and everyone enjoyed the stars. Especially Father Mac, the defrocked Irish priest, and Sister, not abstaining anymore, Bre. However, their stars were in each other's eyes. Then disaster struck once more.

The boat was out of water. No showers, the head was dead, and dishes needed to be tended to. Thinking caps went on and Diamond Dave came to the rescue. River water was gathered for the head and melted water from the ice chests was boiled up to wash dishes. Problem solved -- and the partying continued on into the wee hours of the night. Awakening at 4:30 a.m. Father Mac followed the call of nature out to the

sandbar only to find the Lion King and J, the River Queen, still upright in their chairs by the bonfire, enjoying the outdoors in a dream state.

Morning came and another wonderful breakfast of French toast, strawberries, and champagne was in order. After cleaning up, Happy Go, Sparky, and J, the River Queen, had a hand at fishing, reeling in a variety of river inhabitants.

Alas, all good things must come to an end, so down the river to Port McGregor they went, with Doc Holiday and Nurse-Why-Not-Chirp taking turns at the stern. Securely docked, it was time to unload and move all belongings to awaiting vehicles.

Once more, disaster struck -- with Diamond Dave pulling, and the Lion King pushing, a wagon of coolers and various equipment, which tipped over into the river. The Lion King quickly jumped in for a salvage operation. But soon the water was over his head; and as we all know lions don't swim. So much for a fan and the coffee pot.

What a wonderful weekend. I highly recommend it! By the way, Diamond Dave and Sparky never had a secret. I was just stringing you along. Next month's Mirth will be written in France as we are going for a little vacation...

MUSHROOMS IN WHITE WINE

1/2 lb. baby portabella mushrooms

Salt and fresh ground pepper to taste

1/2 lb. white button mushrooms

2 cups white Chablis wine

1 1/2 sticks butter

1/8 cup chopped parsley

4 large garlic cloves, minced

1 small loaf rustic bread, sliced thick

Clean mushrooms with a damp cloth. Cut mushrooms into bite sized pieces. Melt butter in a large heavy bottomed skillet. Add mushrooms and garlic. Salt and pepper to taste. Sauté over low/medium heat until mushrooms begin to lose their water (about 5-7 minutes). Add more butter if mushrooms begin to absorb too much. Add white wine and bring to a simmer. Cover with a lid just off center so some moisture can escape. Simmer over low heat for 25-30 minutes or until moisture is reduced to half. Sprinkle over and stir. Serve up and have bread ready for sopping up the fragrant juices. Out of this world!

VIVE LA FRANCE

Tapestry Magazine October 2007

As promised, this month's column is about our sojourn in France.

As I write this, I'm sitting in the Marseilles airport waiting to board our plane for the flight home.

Accompanying my wife, Brenda, and me were our son, Conor, and friend Jason Schwarz. We spent three wonderful days in Paris, taking in the usual tourist sites -- what's left of the Bastille; the Cathedral of Notre Dame; part of the Louvre; the Eiffel Tower and the cemetery, Pere Lachaise. (Who in their right minds could be in Paris and not pay their respects to the late Jim Morrison?) The food was outstanding, the wine exquisite, and the French people we met in Paris were extremely gracious.

From Paris we flew to Marseilles, where we were met by our friends from Connecticut, Jack and Sheryl, and Sheryl's cousin, Lisa. A nine-passenger Mercedes Benz van was procured, and we were off to the Villa Clara in the medieval village of St. Jeannette in the French Riviera overlooking the Mediterranean Sea.

Tough life, huh?

But first, a stop in Le Castellet. Sheryl's relatives, Bernard, Annette, Regina and Michael had prepared a feast of massive proportions. It is what Bernard called Couscous. It is what I call Magnificent. A huge pot of couscous was accompanied by a tomato vegetable sauce, grilled chorizo sausage, grilled cumin lamb kabobs, barbequed chicken thighs, and mutton -- so tender it was literally falling apart. And that was just the first course.

Next, we were served a mixed green salad with olive oil and vinegar dressing. Round three involved eight or so giant hunks of different cheeses served with sliced baguettes. And, of course, there was dessert (ice cream and fruit). And coffee. The meal went for hours, and at every turn there was local wine being opened, tasted and consumed. Bernard would occasionally burst into song and everyone would join in heartily. Dancing went on until the wee hours of the morning.

Man, the French know how to throw a party -- and (did I mention?) be extremely gracious.

The next morning (Look Ma, no sulfites in the wine, so no hangover. Oui! Oui!), Regina took us to meet her friend, Yves. Yves then took us to a local vineyard, where the harvest was underway. It was early this year, and there hadn't been any rain for four months -- so the crop would be smaller than usual, too.

I tasted a few grapes, which were simply delicious and incredibly sweet. We then headed to Yves' family winery for taste testing -- and, of course, purchased cases of wine to be appreciated down the road. (Believe me, they were appreciated!).

Our next destination was St. Jeanette, located fifteen kilometers up the mountain from the Mediterranean Sea. We'd made a short stop in Vence to stock up on supplies, first, as we had rented a villa with full cooking facilities for the week. I was at the wheel of a full-sized Mercedes Benz van, complete with straight-stick transmission, as we proceeded up the mountain on a road just wide enough -- barely -- for a couple of Volkswagen Beetles. And, of course, there were bicycles on the right, cars coming at us from the left, and motorbikes slipping between us and the oncoming traffic at 100 kilometers an hour.

I'd never driven in France, didn't know what the road signs meant, and had never been on a traffic "roundabout" -- where there are no stop signs and you just merge into traffic from your road, and then merge out onto the road you want to take. It's not uncommon to have five or six roads dumping into these roundabouts. Apparently pedestrians have the right of way, because it is also not uncommon to have someone step out right in front of you.

Up the mountain we went, switchback after switchback, into the village. My co-pilot, Sheryl, directed me up a tight winding street with barely enough room for the van -- and then informed me that we had gone the wrong way. (It was wrong signage, not the co-pilot's misinterpretation). Remember, this is a clutch situation -- no automatic transmission, no way to go forward, a car behind me, six people yelling directions at me, and I can't see out the back. The car backed down but there was no way to negotiate the van, so I did a three -- no, a 14 --point California turn to get turned around. Jack and Conor bailed and headed for a beer. Great -- now I only had four people yelling directions. We made it down only to find five gorgeous French ladies, all in their eighties, pointing their fingers at me and laughing hysterically.

On to the villa. It was about a third of a mile through town, and it took another 20 minutes of jockeying back and forth, pulling in mirrors, and being the American attraction of the afternoon, to get there. This was definitely the best white-knuckle-experience of my life.

The villa was great -- complete with a pool, outdoor wood-fired oven, and a commanding view of the French Riviera and the Mediterranean Sea. We spent the week relaxing, touring St. Paul de Vence, Nice, Antibes, Cannes, the beach, Monaco, and the Italian Riviera.

Alas, the week passed swiftly and it was time to head back to Sheryl's wonderful cousins' house for round two of What I call Magnificent. That

A huge pot of couscous was accompanied by a tomato vegetable sauce, grilled chorizo sausage, grilled cumin lamb kabobs, barbequed chicken thighs, and mutton -- so tender it was literally falling apart. And that was just the first course.

meal consisted of aperitifs, appetizers (five different pates, black olive tapenade and sturgeon caviar); Grilled Marinated Duck Breast with boiled fresh potatoes swimming in a wonderful beef gravy; Salad Landaise (Mixed greens with fois gras on toast tips). Cheese, of course; and Lemon sorbet in a large brandy snifter, bathed in fresh squeezed lemon and vodka.

The next day we went to Bandol to visit Jean-Yves and Ann, friends of Bernard and Annette. Here, we had round three -- with the first course being Quail with Wild Mushrooms and Grapes and a side of rosemary potatoes. Did I mention anything about the French being a very gracious people?

We loved the entire trip. Au Revoir!

BLACK OLIVE TAPENADE

1/2cup chopped black olives   2 cloves garlic

3/8 cup capers   1 tbl extra virgin olive oil

1/4 cup anchovies   Salt and pepper to taste

Place all ingredients in a blender or food processor. Puree. Spread over your favorite type of cracker or melba toast.

COOKBOOKS

Tapestry Magazine November 2007

I'm not much into material things. Owning stuff doesn't really trip my trigger. And besides, I'm married to the original "Material Girl," so she more than makes up for my deficiency in this matter.

Over the years, however, I have managed to accumulate a few cookbooks. Ok, not just ten or twenty, but maybe five or six hundred or so. They just seem to show up and say "Give me a home." People stop by and say, „"Hey, Jim, my mom went into the nursing home and wants

you to have these cookbooks and her favorite home recipes"; or "I just happened to be at the Spectrum Depot, Goodwill, or a garage sale and found these cookbooks that I knew you couldn't live without." It is, of course, wonderful. I truly live a charmed life. I love to read cookbooks. Brenda (the original "Material Girl") and I have spent many Sunday afternoons sipping a little wine, having some hors d'oeurves, and "oohing and ahhing" over what people have assembled in their cookbooks.

Because I get a lot of cookbooks from wonderful friends, I sometimes lose track of where they have all come from. The other day I ran across a small, yellow, heavy paper cover cookbook called *Corn Country Cooking* by La Verne Keettel Hull. Also, on the top of the cover, it reads *"Souvenir Of Iowa."* I tried to Google information on it but was unable to bring anything up. There is no date or publisher printed on this copy. Because of some of the verbage and recipes, I think it is from the late 1940s or early 1950s.

It's wild! One of the chapters is called "Fish Fry Tonight." The following statements are included:

No. 1. "At Marquette near the Mississippi, a roadside sign advertises 'Fish Bologna,' and people who have tasted it say it's pretty good."

No. 2. "You may even eat Iowa fish at a New York cocktail party -- river carp bits, smoked and fancifully packaged, are a big delicatessen item."

So now, I am curious fivefold:

1. Who is/was La Verne Keettel Hull?

2. Who and when was this book published?

3. Does anyone remember who sold fish bologna at Marquette and/or have a recipe?

4. Who was packaging smoked river carp and distributing it as far as New York?

5. What will my " Material Girl" be in the next life?

If anyone has information they would to share on these questions, you can contact me by email at: Jbmctsw@oneota.net

Or mail me at:

Jim McCaffrey

2138 Twin Springs Road

Decorah, IA 52101

I'd be very grateful to hear from anyone. If I get any response, I will share next month.

Here's a recipe reprinted from *Corn Country Cooking:*

BOLOGNA GRAVY

Make white sauce in top of double boiler, using two tablespoons of melted butter, two tablespoons of flour, and two cups of milk, seasoning the sauce with half a teaspoon of salt, a dash each of Tabasco and Worcestershire sauce.

Into this white sauce goes the meat of a half of a large ring of bologna, which has been peeled and then put through a food chopper.

Combine the meat with sauce, correct the seasoning (this means add more salt if you think so) let simmer over hot water until ready to find places at table.

Men find it habit forming; boys love it. Nobody has ever served it at a ladies' luncheon.

HORSERADISH

Tapestry Magazine December 2007

No matter how he slices it, it's still fish. G.C. (Curly) Sharp of Marquette, Ia., is secretive about the process but he has a store sign which tells all: "It looks like bologna, it tastes like bologna, it has the texture and aroma of bologna, but it's fish." Sharp has been making "the world's first fish bologna" for 17 years. (Barth Photo)

Curly Sharp owned the Marquette Meat and Fish Market and made the original fish bologna.

The following is an excerpt from my cookbook (Midwest Cornfusion) recipe for "Beef and Horseradish Salad":

"Every year we get a few of the boys together and dig horseradish. This process requires cleaning the horseradish in an old agitator washing machine. We then have to peel it all. We use a hand-crank meat grinder to process it to a coarse grated condiment. The fumes will bring tears to your eyes in a couple of minutes. So you grind until you absolutely can't stand it anymore. Then you get up, grab a beer, and someone else takes your place. Repeat the process until done.

Gee, do we know how to have fun? Talk about seeing a bunch of grown men cry! ..."

This year I was unable to participate in our annual horseradish harvest. So I was pleasantly surprised when my good friend, Tom Bockman, stopped me at the local grocery store parking lot and told me that he and the boys had prepared a few jars for me and to stop by and pick them

up. Much to my surprise, Tom had taken time to prepare my horseradish aside of the rest of the batch.

We have two schools of thought when it comes to horseradish preparation. I like my horseradish mixed with white vinegar only. I am, after all, a purist, you know. Tom and his brothers, Mark and Mike, take exception to that. They grew up planting and digging horseradish alongside their dad, Joe. He loved his own prepared horseradish and passed that love onto his children. So they make it Joe's way with white vinegar and sugar.

For years we have debated the merits of each other's condiment creations. The Bockman brothers have family tradition on their side and I'm a shanty Irish cook with great taste buds. It has been a lot of fun camaraderie.

Speaking of fun camaraderie, I received an overwhelming response to my last month's column. Sharon Larson from Dorchester let us in on who LaVerne Kettel Hull was. She wrote a weekly column for the Waukon newspaper, titled "Mrs. Trotting Shoes." Karen Lonning Teaser added that LaVerne -- whose husband,

Leslie Hull, co-owned the paper -- referred to him in her column as "the man whose socks I darn." Everybody said she loved to share recipes and at each Christmas she shared her recipes for Hull House Cookies -- which Keith Pat Sander has generously shared with us.

Sounds like Laverne was a wonderful person who enjoyed life immensely.

Our fish bologna question was answered by Suzanne Pennington. Her father, Curly Sharp, owned the Marquette Meat and Fish Market. He made the original fish bologna. Suzanne also shared an article written about his bologna from the Dubuque Telegraph Herald. It states the store had a sign advertising Fish Bologna with the following verbage: "It looks like bologna, it tastes like bologna, it has the taste and aroma of bologna, but it's fish." He also put together a little green book titled The Original Mississippi River Catfishing Guide. It had recipes like Rabbit sausage, Rabbit Pie, Squirrel with Dumplings,

and how to pluck a duck. Tim Mason e-mailed me a picture of that book. (If anyone knows where I might find a copy, please let me know).

Thanks to all who responded to my questions. I just could not fit everyone in. No one has come up with an answer for my question of "What will my 'Material Girl' be in the next life? Oh well, maybe some questions are better left alone.

By the way, Sharon thought that maybe Marquette should have a fish bologna cookoff in its future.

Anyone from Marquette have an answer to that?

PS. If anybody has some horseradish recipes or tales they would like to share, my e-mail is jbmctsw@oneota.net

Or mail :

Jim McCaffrey

2138 Twin Springs Rd

Decorah, IA 52101

HULL HOUSE COOKIES

Cream 1 cup sugar and 1 cup butter. Add 1 egg and beat. Stir 5 tablespoons sour cream, 3 1/2 cups flour, 1 tsp baking soda, salt and 1 tsp vanilla. Chill overnight, roll out, cut into desired shapes and bake 350 degrees. Frost with lemon juice and powdered sugar.

Thanks Keith!

TAPESTRY MAGAZINE 2008

RISOTTO

Tapestry Magazine January 2008

A h, risotto ... Poor man's rice, something the Italians have elevated to gastronomical heights.

It is a simple, but absolutely marvelous dish. I first tasted it in Naples, Italy when my wife, Brenda, and I traveled there to study pizza.

At our hotel restaurant, Brenda ordered Risotto with Asparagus Tips. It was served on an ornate silver plate. Brenda exclaimed, "Jim, you just have to try this!" I did -- and instantly fell in love. (With risotto, that is. I already had that love thing going with Brenda). If you have never tried risotto, you are in for a magnificent treat!

I really enjoy making risotto. It is a "hands on" type of dish that requires constant attention. A labor of love, one might say. For a party the other night, I made a risotto similar to the one in Naples, but added sliced mushrooms as well. (Recipe to follow). Preparation is the key. I have everything ready to go ahead of time. I start by sautéing chopped onion, sliced mushrooms, and asparagus tips in a combination of extra virgin olive oil and butter. Next on the agenda, I uncork a bottle of Pinot Grigio (a semi-dry white wine) and ceremoniously pour the room temperature vintage into an ice-filled, stemmed glass. (So this is what the phrase "cooking with wine" is all about).

The onions are translucent and the mushrooms have started to lose their water, so it is time to add the rice. Not just any rice, mind you, but arborio rice. A grain of arborio rice is short and fat and has the ability to absorb a tremendous amount of moisture -- which, in turn, allows the rice to retain a great infusion of flavor from the broth it is absorbing. Into the heavy-bottomed skillet simmering with onions, mushrooms and asparagus tips, I add the rice and stir frequently -- stopping occasionally to sip some grape ambrosia.

A thought enters my mind: New Year's Resolutions. Which reminds me of a quote from Mark Twain... "Now is the accepted time to make your annual good resolutions. Next week you can begin paving hell with them, as usual."

But wait. The rice is ready for the next step. I pour a cup or so of Pinot Grigio into the skillet (room temperature only, so the rice does not flake) and refill my glass.

Stirring at a simmer, the rice absorbs the wine in a couple of minutes, faster than most of my Irish drinking buddies after the annual St. Paddy's Day Parade. (I quickly make a pre-New Year's resolution that from here on out, this risotto is on the wagon). I switch to a simmering pot of chicken broth and start adding a ladleful at a time.

A routine is quickly established. Add a ladleful of broth, sip some wine, and stir until broth is absorbed.

Repeat.

During all of this, I recall the classic Henny Youngman resolution: "My wife and I decided when we got married to never go to bed angry with each other. I haven't slept in over 30 years."

Ladle. sip. stir.

I then think that if my wonderful wife, Brenda, would ever make a resolution that would make my day, it would be to get ready to go out in 10-15 minutes. It's kind of like what my dad used to say about my mother: "She's going to late for her own funeral."

Ladle. sip. stir.

I decide to stay with my resolution of the last 35 years, which is to never make a New Year's resolution. It has served me quite well.

Ladle. Sip. Sip. Sip. Slur... Whoops, time to add the parmesan cheese, and serve. Just remember: "A New Year's resolution goes in one year and out the other."

I hope your up and coming year is filled with everything you want out life. Have a great one!

RISOTTO WITH MUSHROOMS AND ASPARAGUS TIPS

8 cups chicken broth

4 tbl extra virgin olive oil

3 tbl butter

1 small onion, finely chopped

20 or so 2-inch asparagus tips

4 ounces sliced common white mushrooms

1 cup white wine

2 cups Arborio rice

1 cup fresh grated parmesan cheese

Salt and fresh ground black pepper to taste

In a pot large enough, bring chicken broth to a simmer. Meanwhile, utilizing a heavy-bottomed skillet, saute onion, asparagus tips and mushrooms over medium heat. When the onion is translucent, add rice and stir until rice has turned opaque or white (about seven minutes). Add white wine and let rice absorb. Continue to stir. This will only take about two minutes. Add a ladleful of chicken broth and let rice absorb, always stirring. Repeat this process until has become creamy, about 20 minutes. You might not use all of the chicken broth. Turn off heat and add parmesan cheese and maybe two to three tablespoons of butter, if you like. Stir thoroughly and serve immediately.

A PIEMAN'S PASSION FOR PIZZA

Tapestry Magazine February 2008

(THE SEED IS SOWN)

My earliest recollection of pizza was when I was eight or nine years old. Our family was living in Cedar Rapids, IA. My Uncle Tom and my Aunt Margaret asked my parents if they could take my older sister, Angie and myself, out to eat. This was a very special event for us. My parents never went out to eat,

much less take their children. It just wasn't a part of our lives. Mom always made the meals and the whole family always sat down and ate together.

My uncle and aunt took us to Shakey's. It was in the late 1950s and Shakey's was the hot new action in town. I remember it being dark and smoky with a guy in a red and white striped suit banging out Dixieland tunes on a stand up piano. There was a window that you could stand up to and watch the pizza being made. For an eight year-old boy, it was an awesome eye-opening wonder. Probably as astounding as Willy Wonka's Chocolate Factory, don't you think? The pizza itself (this being a first time culinary experience for me) definitely gained a lifelong advocate, in me. A pieman's destiny was in a young boy's future.

(A PIEMAN IS BORN)

In the early 1960s our family moved to Decorah, IA., where Mabe's Pizza was the only game in town. Mabel White had started a small pizza operation close to Luther College. In the beginning, pizza was cut with a scissors and a shoebox was the cash register. My sister took me to Mabe's and I never looked back.

It was a place of great camaraderie. Everybody hung out there, so it seemed. Mabe's moved downtown into the space formerly occupied by two restaurants which had operated side by side. Don White, Mabe's son and co-owner by then, hired me when I was a freshman in high school. Not that I was anybody special, mind you, because I think almost every kid in town at that time worked at Mabe's at some point. I, however, worked there for seven years through high school and college.

Mostly, I delivered pizzas. But I still made a lot of pies. A lot of pies! We cooked and pounded out fresh sausage on a fourfoot- wide flat grill and grated fresh mozzarella by hand with flat cheese graters on each pizza. Pretty much everything was made from scratch using fresh ingredients. On weekends, we literally made hundreds of pizzas. We were definitely "Piemen."

(CONTINUING EDUCATION)

I moved to Iowa City and, in 1976, James Ronan and I traveled to southern Europe for seven weeks. Eurorail was the means of transportation. Somewhere in northern Italy, we got off the train and stopped at a pizzeria.

Eureka! This was not the pie we had become accustomed to in the Midwest. This pie had a thin crust, very little topping and was baked in a wood fired brick oven. It was a marvelous revelation in texture and taste.

We moved on to Rome and Venice and devoured pies. We couldn't get enough! Each one was a little different, but excellent in it's own right.

Well, that was thirty years ago. (Gee, I guess that dates Ronan!) Anyway, we started making pizza at the Café Deluxe until we sold the restaurant. They were definitely American-style pizzas. But I have been experimenting ever since. My lovely wife, Brenda, and I have traveled around the U.S. in the last three years to study pizza - - and we went back to Rome and Naples to taste and appreciate Italian "Pies."

Naples is considered the birthplace of modern pizza. In the early 1800s street vendors were hawking flat bread with olive oil and sea salt to workers for lunch. In 1889, a pieman (pizzaiolo), was invited to make pizza for visiting Queen Margherita of Savoy. One pizza was made of tomato, mozzarella, and fresh basil. Red, white and green, the colors of the Italian flag. To this day, it is the favorite pie in Italy, or so I'm told.

"Now that's a Pie."

(WHEN THE MOON HITS YOUR EYE LIKE A BIG PIZZA PIE, THAT'S AMORE!)

Well, I got the bug -- and Brenda did, as well.

So we did what any other sane couple would do in our shoes: We built a 5' by 7' brick-fired oven and are in the process of putting a restaurant around it. We have been working on it on weekends since Thanksgiving.

Scratch that -- mostly we have been shoveling snow. But eventually pizza will come And we hope to share a lifetime love of pie with you as well.

A PIEMAN'S PASSION FOR PIZZA -- BASIC PIZZA

(Makes 2- 12" round pizzas)

Dough

1 1⁄4 oz. pkg dry yeast

1 1/3 cups 85 degree water

4 cups white all purpose flour
  (unbleached)

2 cups tomato sauce

1 minced garlic clove

1 Tbl torn fresh basil

2 oz. sliced pepperoni

3⁄4 lb fresh ground Italian sausage 4 Tbl
  olive oil (Browned and drained) 1tsp salt

12 oz. fresh grated mozzarella cheese

1⁄2 red onion sliced thin

6 oz. sliced mushrooms

Extra virgin olive oil

Salt and fresh ground black pepper

Fresh grated parmesan cheese

Make dough: Dissolve yeast in water until bubbly (five minutes). Add rest of ingredients. Mix and then knead on floured counter for ten minutes, adding a little flour if dough is sticky. Place in large oiled bowl and cover tightly with plastic wrap or wet towel. Let rise until double, 1 1/2-2 hours. Punch down and let rise again.

Combine tomato sauce, garlic and basil for sauce. Saute mushrooms in olive oil until they start to brown. Preheat oven to 475 degrees. Divide dough in half. Roll one half into a 12" circle. Place on a corn meal sprinkled 12" pizza pan. Add 1⁄2 sauce and spread evenly over pizza. Add 1⁄2 remaining ingredients. Repeat with 2nd pizza. Bake 15-20 minutes until crust and cheese is golden brown. Since it is February, surprise the special one in your life and make heart-shaped crusts. Hey, live a little.

BE A PIEMAN!

EMPTY BOWLS
Tapestry Magazine March 2008

My good friend, Sarah Welper, suggested not long ago that I write a column on soup. I said "Sure! Soup is one of my favorite foods to make."

And the timing could not have been more appropriate. On March 16, 2008, an intrepid group of pot throwers, bread builders, soup creators, and community volunteers will descend upon the Luther College Center For the Arts in Decorah, IA. The event is the third annual "Empty Bowls" project. For those not knowledgeable of this event, it is a fundraiser to help support local food closets and efforts to fight world hunger.

Here's how it works. Local potters have created 1000 soup bowls. Local organizations, restaurants, and private individuals will bake bread and make soup. For a mere 20 dollars, you pick out a soup bowl of your choice, select soup and bread, and sit down for a wonderful time of sharing with friends and strangers. And don't forget to have seconds. The bowl is yours to take home. Use it as a reminder of the many empty bowls throughout the world where hunger exists. And while you are at it, bring along a few of your friends (10 or 20 or so) to join in and make this "Empty Bowls" project a rousing success.

If you live outside the Decorah area, I'm inviting you to come and join us as well. It's a wonderful experience and a great way to wave this long winter away! Last year the project had 25 completely different soups (and breads as well) to choose from. There will be something for everyone.

This is my second year of participation in this

project. Last year I made Pasta and Fagioli soup. This is a wonderful peasant soup from Italy consisting of mostly pasta pieces and cannelloni beans with chicken stock, tomatoes, and maybe a ham hock or two, etc. It probably originated from weekend leftovers on the same basis as red beans and rice in Cajun/Creole country. This year it is time for something new. Actually two new soups, thus the title of this month's column. I'm thinking something robust and earthy like a Cajun gumbo and something lighter like a Greek lemon rice soup.

Both are fun to make and delightful to eat. No! Wait! Maybe a tortilla soup or a potato and leek soup. I'm vacillating. I can't decide. If anybody out there has a soup they absolutely can't live without and wish to share with our Tapestry readers, you can email me at jbmctsw@oneota. net. I am always up for new recipes and the "Empty Bowls" project can always use another unique soup. In fact, here's a way for you to get involved as well. I was going to make two soups, but if readers respond and send in recipes, I'll choose a recipe and make that as well.

WOW! 15 gallons of soup, no waiting. Now, it will be "Three Soups For Sister Sarah!" Thanks for taking to time to read this column and hear my passion to fight world hunger. There is just no excuse for it. The following is an excerpt from my cookbook Midwest Corn Fusion. Let us help the whole world to dance, and to hunger no longer.

"DANCE LIKE NOBODY'S WATCHING"

I wanted to create a soup that was infused with some of my favorite flavors. Every ingredient in this soup adds its own unique taste and the outcome is just out of sight. It certainly didn't last very long at my house.

A good rustic bread for dipping brings it all together. Serves 12-16.

- 4 qts. chicken broth (homemade or store-bought)
- Juice of one lime
- 8 oz. 30-40 count uncooked shrimp, peeled and deveined
- 2 lbs small red potatoes
- 2 lbs hot Italian sausage links

- 2 oz. fresh basil, shredded
- 1 red onion, chopped
- Salt and fresh ground black pepper
- 4 cloves garlic, minced
- 4 oz. fresh or frozen green beans, French cut

Boil potatoes in a large pot until just tender. Drain and let cool. In the meantime, grill or pan fry sausages. Take off heat and let cool. Dice potatoes and thinly slice sausages. Pour chicken broth in a large pot. Bring to a boil. Add potatoes, sausage, onion, garlic, green beans, and lime juice. Simmer for five minutes. Add shrimp and basil. Simmer another 3-4 minutes until shrimp turns pink. Do not overcook or shrimp will become tough. Add salt and pepper to taste and serve immediately.

THE "ART" OF COOKING

Tapestry Magazine April 2008

Perhaps a better title to this month's column would be The "Art" of cooking. For those of you who haven't heard or didn't know him, Art Hoppin passed away on March 13, 2008. It was a tremendous loss for our community. He was 57 years young. I want to share with you some fond memories of the man I consider my mentor in the culinary profession.

I moved back to Decorah, IA from Madison, WI in September, 1978. My cousin, Terry Carolan, was remodeling the Montgomery Building into a mini mall and had asked me to help out. This is where I first met Art.

He had incredible and wonderful blue eyes; they always reminded me of Terrance Hill in the "Trinity" movies. Always a twinkling sparkle. Accompanying those great eyes was his mischievous smile. It was always like he knew something you didn't know. And he probably did.

One thing that Art absolutely did know was food and food preparation.

I got my first glimpse of his abilities when Brenda and I attended Art and Karla Presler's wedding in the spring of 1979. They had met at Luther College and built a house on a wonderful wooded property north of Decorah. When we arrived, Art had been up half the night roasting a whole hog. I thought to myself, this guy is into some serious cooking. Awesome!

Of course, it was accompanied by all of the trimmings. He and Karla put out a fantastic feast for all of their guests.

Paul Sofranko started the Café Deluxe in the Montgomery Building; and in the spring of 1981, Brenda and I (and another friend, Dean Thuente, for a short while) purchased the Café Deluxe. Art was working the evening shift and Karla was baking. The Café Deluxe was where real gourmet cooking began in Decorah, in my humble opinion. Mark Smeby, the morning chef [and current co-owner, with his wife, Joanie, of Decorah's La Rana Bistro -- another terrific venue. Ed.], was creating fantastic soups and Karla and Amy Wilkinson (George) were baking wonderful artisan breads, whole wheat cinnamon rolls and all sorts of desserts. Remember those cheesecakes? And, of course, Art was making his magic at night with a couple of specials not to be found at any of the local steakhouses.

Working with Art was just pure pleasure. He never got flustered. He always had the right way of explaining a cooking procedure. He was never condescending, only happy to share his knowledge. Working together, it was almost like a choreographed dance. He was amazingly dedicated to the Café Deluxe and to its customers. If he had an order ready and the wait staff didn't get it out to the customer almost immediately, Art was hustling the order out. Needless to say, the wait staff quickly learned what Art expected of them. And they all loved him for it. He made each one of us a better person.

I'd like to think his dedication to the Café Deluxe was what made his decision to snowshoe out a mile or so to the highway for a Saturday shift during a miserable snowstorm, but I think the possibility of being able to catch the Iowa Hawkeye basketball game on his little TV in the Café's kitchen was the true motivation. Art loved the Hawkeyes. Many a night we were cooking and either moaning or cheering them on.

He also loved feeding the masses. We decided that for Nordic Fest we would serve up an old fashioned BBQ. We had John Beard build us an outside grill out of a 220-gallon oil tank. We made BBQ chicken with our secret sauce, homemade potato salad and fresh sweet corn on the cob. People lined up for blocks. It was wild.

When Saturday nights started to get a little slow, Art and I decided to compete a little with the local steakhouses. We offered an eight-ounce ribeye steak, baked potato, salad and a glass of wine for $4.95. The first night we sold 142 steaks in three hours. Art cooked them all on our small four-foot grill. Talk about a workout.

When the downstairs of the Montgomery building became available, Art, Karla, Brenda, and I made the decision to expand. We wanted to be able to give more of our employees full time status. Even though Brenda and I had our names on the bank loans, McCaffrey's belonged to all of us. Especially, the kitchen was Art's. He designed all of the menu items and laid out the kitchen just like he wanted it. It was a great menu, with gourmet items at that time – like shrimp scampi, veal parmesan, and fresh made chicken cordon bleu. We also started making a once weekly special using a different country's cuisine. So in addition to our regular menu, we added four three-course meals for each cuisine. Art was incredible in his ability to master the nuances of each area's cuisine.

I am truly blessed to have had the experience

of sharing life with Art in the kitchen for the three or four years I did. I would like to think he taught me well -- not only about kitchen skills, but also about values and how to treat your fellow man.

Karla called me up and asked me if I would cook for the Memorial gathering. I was humbled and felt honored at the same time. We decided on a menu of which I'm sure Art would have approved: Chicken Creole, Red Beans and Rice, Regular and also Green Chile Cornbread. Karla said she had corn from her and Art's garden. We added it to the cornbread so we could all share a last meal with Art. On the morning before the gathering, I called Karla. She said "You just can't believe it, Jim. I have 35 robins, seven bluebirds and some blue jays out on the lawn." I said, "It has to be a sign." She said, "I think so, too."

We love you, Art, and will miss you dearly.

GREEN CHILE CORNBREAD

1 1/2 cups buttermilk

1 4 oz can diced green chiles

1 large white onion, diced

2 cloves garlic, minced

1 cup yellow cornmeal

1 cup white flour

2 tsp. sugar

1 tbl baking soda

1 tsp baking powder

1 tsp salt

2 large eggs

1 cup sharp cheddar cheese, grated

Preheat oven to 400 degrees. Put buttermilk, chiles, onion, and garlic in saucepan and cook over low heat for 5-6 minutes, stirring often. Let cool for 15 minutes. Mix cornmeal, flour, baking soda and powder, and salt in a large bowl. Beat eggs and add buttermilk mixture and cheese. Fold into cornmeal mixture and mix until just blended. Try not to overdo mixing so the batter stays light. Pour into a greased 1 1/2 quart baking dish and bake for 40-45 minutes until golden brown. Test with a toothpick. Cornbread is ready when toothpick comes out clean from the center.

AS EASY AS (TOMATO) PIE

Tapestry Magazine May 2008

The long, hard winter has finally released its tenacious grip on the hills and valleys of Northeast Iowa.

Time to turn to the gardens, turn the soil, and turn to the temptations of nature's love apple, the tomato.

Part of enduring that long hard winter was the inevitable parade of non-palatable orbs of pallid fruit which are the standard fare of at least small town market fare in the upper Midwest. Even the hothouse tomatoes are picked green and have no flavor. What is wrong with this picture? My mama did not raise this boy to be no fool. This is not as nature intended!

But I digress. The exquisite lure of a slice of fresh-grown tomato, lightly salted and seasoned with fresh, ground black pepper, makes the trials of one's garden preparation and maintenance just faint springtime memories. Talk about heaven on earth! Add some crisp new cucumber and thinly sliced onion on hearty rye -- that's definitely my sandwich of choice for the entire year.

Of all of nature's foods, the tomato, in my mind, has to be one of the most versatile. I mean, the logistics of whipping a watermelon across the garden at your kid brother's turned back seem nearly impossible. On the other hand, a tomato..? Seriously, the tomato plays an important part of the cuisines in most of the world. Think of the multitude of Italian sauces; a French bouillabaisse; Latin American salsas (where, incidentally, the tomato is believed to have originated); American barbeque; Lebanese kebabs -- and even Key West, Florida, for a thick slice of beefsteak on Jimmy Buffet's Cheeseburger in Paradise.

Let's climb the ladder of tomato tales. I know as a child I sat on a bushel of tomatoes. Hey, I just wanted to be the straw boss. My parents gardened as long as I can remember and tomatoes were king. Dad had seven gardens and was one of the original members of Decorah's Farmers Market. My mother didn't really can tomatoes but made tomato juice laced with hot peppers and froze it in 1/2 gallon paper milk cartons. Everyone would save containers for her and she, in turn, would pass out juice for the remainder of the year. She had a large chest-type freezer and it seemed most of it was filled at the end of the season with that wonderful frozen concoction (sorry, Jimmy). Brenda and I got together many weekends with her brother-in-law and sister, Luther and Karen Anderson, to make and can homemade salsa. OH MY!

One year, my good friend, Tom Tofte and I decided we would be tomato kings and painstakingly planted 100 plants. A hole was dug for each with a tablespoon or two of Epsom salt at the bottom. We pruned all the leaves except the top two or three and buried each plant to the top two inches. The stalk became a huge root. We tamped the ground, spread newspapers for weed cover and either caged or staked each plant. It was a labor of love. We had flowers and green tomatoes up the ying-yang ... All right! Then we had rain up the ying-yang ... Oh no! And, of course, we got tomato blight up the ying-yang... Darn! Let me tell you, "Tomato pauperism is not all it is cracked up to be."

In recent years I have become enchanted with heirloom tomatoes. Another great friend, Diane Ott Whealey out at SeedSavers Exchange, has brought my tomato knowledge to wonderful enlightenment. Tomatoes with such exotic names as Brandywine, Cherokee Purple – and my favorite, German Pink, have become standard fare at our table. Just delicious! If you haven't been out to SeedSavers Heritage Farm, by all means put it at the top of your list of priorities for the spring. You will be pleasantly surprised. It is a wonderful organization that is helping to change the world for the better, each and every day. And the tomatoes aren't too shabby either.

For an easy salsa recipe, see below; and stay tuned for our next thrilling episode, titled "When Good Tomatoes Go Bad!"...

AS EASY AS (TOMATO) PIE FRESH TOMATO SALSA AND CHIPS

3-4 lbs of fresh ripe tomatoes, diced

1 large red onion, diced fine

1 large green pepper, diced fine

4-6 cloves garlic, minced

4-6 jalapenos, de-veined, de-seeded and minced

2 limes

salt and fresh ground black pepper

Tortilla chips of your choice

You can put this together right away, in the container that you are serving the salsa in. Just make sure the bowl is large enough to hold all of the ingredients and there is enough room to mix. Combine the tomatoes, onion green pepper, garlic, and jalapenos. Slice limes in half. Use a fork to help squeeze out the lime juice by twisting the lime pulp (called forking your lime). Add this to the salsa and stir. Now add salt and pepper to taste. I like to refrigerate for a couple hours. It really helps the different flavors meld together. For hotter salsa don't de-vein or de-seed the jalapenos.

FAWN AND JIM'S EXCELLENT ADVENTURE:
(THE QUEST FOR THE STAFF OF LIFE)

Tapestry Magazine June 2008

Jim and Fawn in Grand Marais, MN, learning to bake bread.

As some of you may know, our family is building a restaurant/bakery on what is left of the family farm next to Twin Springs Park in Decorah, IA.

We have constructed a 5x7 foot wood-fired oven which will have a twofold purpose. First we fire the oven up to 750 degrees on the floor and 900 degrees at the dome ceiling which is 16 inches above the floor. When operating the restaurant we can bake a pizza in about 90 seconds. Second, after we've finished making pizzas for the day, we let the fire die out and pull out the ashes.

When the oven floor temperature drops to 650 degrees we mop it out so that we have a clean floor to bake bread on.

So all is right with the world, right?

Not quite so fast, my friends. It seems if you are going to bake bread, you probably should have someone who knows how to do it. Especially at 650 degrees! A plan was hatched; go to the worldwide web, type in "Sourdough Bread Baking In A Wood Fired Oven" and see what opportunities were to be had. I found a school in Maine, two in San Francisco, and one in Kentucky.

Hmmm. This involves driving, sitting in airports for hours on end, renting cars, etc. etc. etc. There had to be a better solution... EUREKA! Further research finds The North House Folk School in Grand Marais, Minnesota. I call them and find out the class is full, and the next class is in six months. I plead my case to squeeze into the upcoming class, but there are already two people ahead of me on the waiting list.

A solution is conceived. A second class would be held the following week. I said, "Great, sign us up for two people!" One week before the class is set to begin I get a call that it has been canceled. Not enough response to warrant a second class. Fortunately, our instructor, Amy James, is a wonderful person and she agrees to conduct an abbreviated class. ALL RIGHT ... ROAD TRIP! We make a company decision that Fawn -- my daughter [not by blood, but by something deeper and richer -- LOVE] and my good friend, as well -- and myself will take the class.

I called my sister, Angie, in St Paul to arrange a get-together and an over-night stay [to break up the eight-hour drive] We agree to meet in Hudson, Wisconsin at The Brick Oven for pizza. This is the closest I have found to authentic-style pizza found in Naples Italy (the alleged birthplace of pizza). As always, the pizza is fabulous, topped with water buffalo mozzerella, which is sweeter and creamier than beef mozzarella. This pizza alone is worth the three-hour trip! We then followed Angie back to St. Paul to Cossetta's, a family-run Italian restaurant and grocery since the 1920s. I wanted to pick up a block of fresh asiago cheese to experiment with in some of the bread we would be baking. And, of course, we couldn't resist buying some of Cossetta's also wonderful pizza for a late night snack to share with Angie's husband, Mark.

Did I mention that his last name is Cosimini? And did I mention that he is of Italian descent with a magnificent sense of humor? We spent a couple of hours bandying back and forth possible names for our up-coming restaurant and believe it or not we came up with a name that everyone really likes. McCaffrey's Dolce Vita (the sweet life) and Twin Springs Bakery. FANTASTIC! It has only been two years of inability to reach a consensus on a name. WHEW!

Early in the morning, after coffee with Mark and Angie, Fawn and I embark for Grand Marais. A brief stop in Duluth and lunch in Two Harbors. Neither of us had ever been to the North Shore of Lake Superior; it is definitely a must see. Absolutely breathtaking. We arrive at the North House Folk School at 3 p.m. and are immediately greeted by our enthusiastic teacher, Amy James. We dig right into the crust of the matter. Amy starts throwing out baking terminology -- words like autolyse, preferment, lame, and poolish. I look at Fawn and her eyes are glazed like a deer in a car's headlights. Lucky for us, there are only three in our class and Amy could take time to help us struggle through it all. We make preferment and start a sponge for some sourdough wheat and rye bread. Day 2, we we start at eight a.m. and end at 5:15 p.m. We baked focaccia, sourdough wheat and rye, ciabatta, forgasse, and and a sourdough with wild rice. We shared focaccia, along with smoked salmon and lake trout, with a multitude of people taking other classes as well. Wonderful cameradie! I highly recommend looking at the school's website <www.northhousefolkschool.com> and participating in a class. Just a really fun experience. Amy was just an incredible teacher and neat person. And the bread wasn't too shabby, either. Thanks, Amy!

SIMPLE FOCACCIA

1 1/4 cups warm water	1 tsp salt
2 T olive oil	2 tsp instant yeast
4 cups flour	1 cup sourdough starter
1 tsp sugar	

Mix water and starter. Add the olive oil, yeast, sugar and salt. Mix well. Add flour 1/2 cup at a time until dough forms a rough ball and pulls away from the sides of the bowl.

Turn on a lightly floured surface. Knead until smooth, adding sprinkles of flour if sticky. Place in a greased bowl. Cover with plastic wrap and let rise one hour. Degas and turn on a lightly floured surface. Shape into one large or two smaller rounds. Roll out to 1/2 inch thickness. Place on a cookie sheet or peel generously sprinkled with semolina. Cover and let rise 30-45 minutes. Uncover. Pour 1 T olive oil on round. Using fingertips, gently spread oil over surface of the loaf. Then use fingertips to make deep indentations over the entire surface of the loaf. Sprinkle with your choice of toppings. (Basil, oregano, onion, garlic, sea salt etc.)

At home bake on cookie sheet or baking stone at 425 degrees for 20-30 minutes.

EAT UP!

A ROUSING CHEER TO THE STINKY ROSE

Tapestry Magazine July 2008

A rose by any other name is still a rose ... unless it is a stinky rose.

Then it is the favorite of chefs from all over the world, GARLIC! (Except Norway, of course. But hey, they do have lutefisk).

And I'm not talking garlic powder, garlic salt, dehydrated minced garlic, etc. We are reaching for the whole enchilada. No time for being namby-pambies here. We are going to step out into a brave new world, reach into the depths of our souls and immediately proceed to the produce department of our local grocery store or food co-op.

When a slightly acrid and pungent odor tickles your nostrils, the road to garlic nirvana is within your reach. While not claiming to be a Gaelic garlic guru, I shall attempt to disperse a few tidbits of somewhat useful information (Stinky Rose 101) on selecting the proper bulb for your dining delight.

Number one: Do not be tempted or seduced into the easy path of buying a jar of preminced garlic. Even though the work is already accomplished for you, the end result is an inferior taste. I don't know exactly why, but this preparation somehow takes the edge off the delicious complexity of fresh garlic. To my taste, it is bland in comparison.

Number two: Opt for the garlic in the bulk bins, if possible. The bulbs in boxes are way more expensive. Plus the boxes don't do anything for the environment, do they?

Number three: When selecting cloves of garlic, always go for the bulbs where the cloves are tightly bonded together. If the cloves are separating, it is an indication that the bulb is not as fresh and may not last as long as one would like.

Number four: If you have trepidations about the robust flavor of regular garlic, try some elephant garlic, if available. The cloves are usually much larger (3-4 to a bulb) and it definitely has a milder taste. OK. Now we are ready to rock and roll. There is a simple and easy way to remove the skin from a clove of garlic. Just lay the clove down on your cutting surface. Take a broad bladed knife, such as a chef's knife, lay it flat side on top of the clove, and WHACK, SMASH, or SLAM the blade with the bottom of your fist. (This really helps to soothe pent up frustrations).

Remove the knife and delicately pick out the paper skin. Now you can commence to mince the clove and take on the world of savory garlic-inspired cuisine.

Maybe start with an easy garlic bread. Pre-heat the oven to about 350 degrees. Slice a loaf of crusty French bread or a baguette in half the long way. Heat over low heat for a couple minutes or so a mixture of about 1/3 to 1/2 cup of extra virgin olive oil and 2 cloves of minced garlic. You are actually "perfuming" the oil with garlic essence.

Turn off the heat. Use a pastry brush and spread the oil mixture onto the cut sides of the bread. If you like, you can sprinkle some salt or fresh grated parmesan cheese on top. Bake for 8-10 minutes or until browned. Slice into inch pieces and serve it piping hot. You will be amazed at how fast it disappears. (This is also so easy that I know even James Ronan can handle it.)

If you like a milder taste, leave the bulb whole and cut off the exposed ends of the cloves. Place on some aluminum foil with cut-clove ends up and drizzle with some olive oil. Encase with the foil and bake in the oven for 40 minutes at 350 degrees. When it has cooled, squeeze out each clove and mix with your olive oil. Spread this mixture on your bread and bake. The roasting mellows the garlic. It is just heavenly! GO GARLIC! I leave you with one of Brenda's favorite garlic recipes.

CHICKEN WITH FORTY CLOVES OF GARLIC

2 cut-up chickens, 3 1/2 pounds each

1 cup olive oil

3 large carrots, peeled and sliced thin

4 stalks celery sliced thin

Salt and pepper

40 cloves garlic, unpeeled

1 1/2 cups dry white wine

Juice of 1 large lemon

1 bunch fresh parsley

1 loaf rustic French bread, sliced
  into rounds

Wash chicken and pat dry with paper towels. Coat with olive oil and brown on all sides in a heavy duty skillet. Place on paper towels to absorb excess oil.

In a large metal casserole, spread out carrots and celery. Salt and pepper chicken to taste on one side. Place that side down in casserole on top of carrots and celery. Salt and pepper to taste on the remaining side. Stuff garlic cloves in and around chicken. Cover tightly with heavy duty aluminum foil. Bake at 375 degrees for 30-40 minutes until chicken juices run clear.

When chicken is about done, place French bread slices on a cookie sheet and put into oven to toast (about 10 minutes). Pull out when toasted brown. When chicken is ready, take out of oven and place on platter with garlic to one side. Cover and keep warm. Place casserole on top of stove, add wine and simmer. Scrape bottom of pan (deglaze) and reduce wine by half, to about 3/4 cup. Add lemon juice and reduce a little more. Divvy up chicken on plates. Pour some sauce over and garnish with parsley. Squeeze garlic cloves on toast and eat away!

MEET ME AT THE FARMERS' MARKET

Tapestry Magazine, August 2008

I have a confession to make. I did not put in a garden this year. In fact, the last couple of years have been a little light as well. I would go out with my good friend, Morgan, to Seed Savers and purchase heirloom tomatoes, peppers, and a variety of veggies and herbs. Together with my stepson Shanon and grandson Kamran, we would get everything planted. But Morgan, Shanon, and Kamran ended up

tending the garden for the rest of the summers. I guess working 50 or so hours a week, doing book signings and catering on weekends has left me with little time as of late. Oh, and did I mention we are also building a restaurant?

There is no rest for the IRISH!

So, the obvious solution to my garden deficient lifestyle is to enlist someone who takes gardening to the next level. That someone (someones actually) is my son Conor and his good friend Sara. I think Conor has inherited his grandfather Leonard's green thumb. He brought over some fresh onions, kohlrabi and green scallions the other day. Wow, out of sight!

This was in the last week of July and he told me that his and Sara's tomato plants were seven feet tall and the German Pinks were larger than softballs. Made me start to salivate.

When we need fresh local produce that Conor and Sara do not have, Brenda and I make haste down to the farmer's market in Decorah, IA. This is a cornucopia of fresh fruits, jams, vegetables organic meats, breads, pastries, eggs and, let us not forget, fresh cut flowers. Brenda spends enough money on these flowers to finance the economy of a small nation. You should see

the flower vendor's grin from ear to ear when Brenda arrives on the scene. It really is one of the highlights of my week when we get to go to the market.

I appreciate all of the effort the vendors have put in. The camaraderie is to just die for. Everyone gets to know you and you get to know them. A lot of laughs are shared and stories told. In the last few weeks I have purchased some wonderful free range chickens and organic steaks. It reminds me of growing up on the farm and raising and butchering our own beef, pork and chickens. You just cannot beat it. I appreciate the farmer's market so much that I dedicated a chapter to it in my cookbook, Midwest Cornfusion. I decided to include in this month's column the lead-in to that chapter. I hope you get a kick out of it.

FLIM FLAMMING AT THE FARMERS MARKET

Hoe! Hoe! Hoe! It's like Christmas in July. Just when you think you have opened your last present, Dad pulls out the red Radio Flyer wagon from behind the couch. (I have visions of sugar snap peas dancing in my head).

At the farmers market, a person can walk right up and look straight into the eye of a red potato and say "I'm going to boil you, baby, and slather you with butter." Carrots are screaming "Julienne me, Julienne me!" A hot tomato and a cool cucumber looking for a good time, a fresh garlic clove, and a couple of naked onions will make an olive oil orgy on a bed of lettuce that will make you think you have died and gone to heaven.

Live a little. Take a fruit loop around the strawberries, cherries, blueberries, apples peaches and plums. Hey, salivate with the sweet corn. And never underestimate the importance of being a kohlrabi. Even brussel sprouts know how to have a good time. (Remember that slathered butter thing).

Seriously, it's always been a special treat for me to attend a farmer's market and be surrounded by all of the fresh produce, flowers, baked goods, herbs, and nowadays, even organic meats and cheeses. The smells are outstanding and the camaraderie can't be beat. So high-tail it down to your local market and let the slathering begin.

Here is a recipe from the above chapter that originally was my Moms and I tinkered a little with for my own taste. Great for picnics and BBQs.

GERDA'S POTATO SALAD

5 lbs. Russet or Idaho potatoes
6 radishes, sliced fine
1 dozen large eggs
4 garlic cloves, minced
1 small red onion, diced fine

1 1/2 cups mayonaise
4 large stalks of onion, diced fine
1/3 to 1/2 cup yellow or Dijon mustard
2-3 large dill pickles, diced fine
Salt and fresh ground black pepper

Peel potatoes and dice into fork-size chunks. Boil until just tender. Drain and cool completely. Boil eggs until hard boiled and allow to cool. Remove shells. Separate yolks from whites and place yolks in a medium sized bowl. Mash yolks into small pieces and stir in garlic, mayonnaise, and mustard. Chop egg whites into small even pieces and add to a large mixing bowl. Stir in potatoes, onion, celery and pickles. Gently stir in mayonnaise mixture until combined. Season with salt and pepper to taste. Refrigerate for 3-4 hours. Potato salad like this tastes best when served very cold.

Thanks, Mom!

NACHO NACHO MAN

Tapestry Magazine September 2008

A couple of summers ago, one of our good friends (and a stonemason), Scott Hawthorn, called and asked me if I had room to store two dump truck loads of limestone building rock.

Platteville stone, you know. Some of the best stone in the area for masonry use. The footings for the new Gunderson Clinic in Decorah were being dug and this great rock could be had for the cost of having it hauled.

Ok, so I'll take two loads myself. You just never know when 30 or so tons of rock will come in handy. When we decided to build our new restaurant, I incorporated this rock into the exterior design.

The time came for laying up the stone and all of the stonemasons were busy and had more work than they could handle. So being Irish, I decided that we would do it ourselves. I mean, how hard could it be? So we applied mesh around the building where the stone would go and my son, Conor, brown coated it with mortar. So far so good. Conor and I and my nephew, Jordan, picked out the first stone, a little gem that only weighed about four to five hundred pounds. We solved the problem of moving it about two hundred feet by loading it on my grandson, Kamran's, radio flyer wagon and carefully, oh so carefully, pulling it into the great final resting place. We applied mortar to the back side and with a Herculean effort picked that bad boy up and set it in place. Whew!

Our salvation came in the form of two brothers from a little town near Guadalajara, Mexico. They had moved to the United States over twenty years ago and worked as masons in California.

They currently reside in Faribault, MN, and were working on building a new ethanol plant over by New Hampton, IA. Rob Sweet, another good friend of ours, was working with them and asked if they could give us a hand. John and Ignacio (better known as Nacho) gave us what was to become Nacho's standard line -- "No problem." Actually, it was many hands, because they showed up with sons, daughters and friends and we had some of our work crew there as well.

So for three Saturdays in July, John and Nacho set stone, their crew cleaned mortar, and the Irish contingent mostly did the grunt work of mixing mortar and hauling stone. I actually got to work with Nacho a lot. We would lift these monster stones in place, squeeze the applied mortar against the brown coated mesh and put in a couple of small shims to help keep the rock in place. I just could not believe these big stones would just stay in place. Parts of the façade were eight feet high and we were not stacking this stone but setting it vertically. "No problem," Nacho would say as he would refresh himself with a sip of Bud Light. Absolutely one of the requirements of weekend stone masonry work is to always have a cooler of cold beer on hand. After seeing the beautiful work these guys did, I became a believer.

It was a bit of a trick to put this façade together. The stone is all shapes and sizes and one must pick and choose the right piece. It was like putting together a huge jigsaw puzzle but more complicated as there wasn't any pattern to follow. For good measure, we also threw in some fossils and other interesting rocks. If you get a chance to stop by when we open in a couple of weeks I think you will love the result of John and Nacho's labor. It was hard work but very enjoyable. The camaraderie was outstanding. Every one was teasing each other just like they were old buddies. The Mexicans and the Irish came together to erect a great wall and became great friends as well. "No problem."

LETTUCE-WRAPPED SHRIMP TACOS

2 lbs 50-60 count cooked shrimp, peeled and de-veined

3-4 avocados, peeled, diced, and soaked in the juice of one lemon

2 heads Romaine lettuce, bottoms removed

Greek Sauce Salsa

2 small cucumbers, peeled

2 medium tomatoes, diced

1/2 medium onion, diced

1 1/4 cups plain yogurt

1 green pepper, diced

2 Tbl olive oil

4 garlic cloves, minced

3 jalapenos, seeded, minced

Juice of one lemon

Juice of one lime

2 tsp. dried dill weed

Salt and fresh ground black pepper

Mix all Greek sauce ingredients together and salt and pepper to taste. Refrigerate for two hours. Do the same with the salsa. When ready to serve, have guests take a lettuce leaf and lay some shrimp in it. With some Greek sauce and add some salsa. Garnish with avocado, wrap up and eat away!

THE MAKING OF A MENU

Tapestry Magazine November 2008

It is a daunting task to conceive and design a new restaurant. One of the hundreds of tasks is to create a menu to fit in the entire scheme of things.

Our new restaurant, "McCaffrey's Dolce Vita" (The Sweet Life), opened on Oct. 1. I wanted to make a menu that was both unique but also simple. So I started by creating the "Dolce Vita" bible -- or in other words, by writing down the recipes of everything we make. I'm

one of the worst when it comes to creating a new dish, going "Boy, this tastes great" -- and the next day forgetting, exactly, how I made it. This is pretty important, though, since almost all of our food is made from scratch.

Since we are making wood-fired pizza, two ingredients are highly important: the crust and the sauce. When Fawn and I went to Grand Marais to study artisan bread-making in a wood-fired oven, we brought back some sourdough starter, also known as chef. I incorporated the chef into my own organic flour dough recipe and we now have a crust very similar to the ones we've had in Italy.

Our primary pizza sauce is tomato-based. I've added fresh roasted garlic, fresh basil and dried oregano along with our top-secret spices. (Sorry, can't tell, it would ruin all of the mystique.) For pizza toppings we have all of the usual suspects plus we came up with some specialty pizzas like Thai Kickin' Chicken with a spicy peanut sauce and the Dolce Vita Salmon Delight, using our own smoked salmon on top of cream cheese with red onions, capers, dill and fresh grated parmesan cheese. And we rounded it out with a Greek pizza and the classic Margherita (my personal favorite).

So, on to appetizers. A few years back my good friend, Bruce Pierce, took me to a Vietnamese restaurant in Des Moines called Ah Dong's. He introduced me to spring rolls and I was hooked. They are similar to an eggroll but a thin wheat flour paper is used for the wrap and our version is served cold. It is stuffed with shrimp, bean sprouts, carrots, radish, green onions and cucumbers and rounded out with a hoisin chile dipping sauce.

We also used my cookbook recipe for stuffed mushrooms and decided to add a traditional Italian appetizer, bruschetta. We finished the appetizer list with a baked jalapeno popper. My fellow food columnist, Jeff Severson, wrote about a similar item, in his column; and one night, a friend of ours, Jeff Leeps, brought in some half-sliced jalapenos stuffed with cream cheese and wrapped in bacon. We immediately threw them into a cast iron skillet and then into the wood-fired oven they went. We altered the recipe a bit by adding garlic, lemon juice, and parmesan cheese to the stuffing, wrapping it with prosciutto and adding a raspberry dipping sauce.

Salads are always in demand. We decided on a house salad based on mixed organic greens with grape tomatoes, cucumbers, carrots, green and black olives, strawberries and black grapes. It's served with our homemade balsamic raspberry vinaigrette. We put a traditional Caesar salad on with homemade dressing and croutons. We finished salads with a country Greek salad with organic mixed greens as a base for fresh tomatoes, thin sliced red onions, Kalamata olives, green pepper, and feta cheese. Top that with our own olive oil and fresh lemon dressing.

Ok folks, this column will eventually end. Bear with me. Sandwiches are next. When we used to prepare for "Live on Winnebago" (a food and arts street festival that was held for several years in Decorah -- Ed.) we served a garlic meatball po' boy with an amber beer and onion gravy which went over well. So it was selected for the menu. A good friend, Paul, told me about the original New Orleans po' boy which was fired potatoes, onions, and Creole seasoning on a French baguette. We tried it and added green peppers, mushrooms, smoked provolone and the traditional po' boy fixings. Number two sandwich hits the menu.

We served food at an art fair last winter with a lemon chicken, smoked provolone, fresh tomato, red onion and garlic aioli on cracked wheat. So number three sandwich was easy. I fell in love with gyros (a Mideastern specialty -- Greek, you know) when I lived in Madison, WI, thirty years ago. It is a mixture of beef and lamb heavily spiced with oregano, baked in our own kitchen and served on pita bread with red onions sliced tomatoes and our homemade tzatziki (cucumber and yogurt sauce).

Three of the four entrees/pastas are adaptations of my recipes from my cookbook *Midwest CornFusion*. They are Chicken Creole, Seafood Manicotti, and Capellini (angel hair pasta with sautéed fresh tomatoes, onions, garlic and fresh basil. The fourth entrée is a Mediterranean Pasta which Mike Domine, our head chef, put together. Sautéed garlic, red onions, kalamata olives, tomatoes, sweet red peppers, mushrooms, basil and feta cheese tossed with linguine and finished with a blush red raspberry vinaigrette.

We also have at least one homemade soup every day, fresh desserts, and a McChildren's menu.

Oh, and did I mention, a beer and wine menu as well.

I am going to leave you with a recipe I concocted for Seed Savers' Harvest Celebration a couple weeks ago. Feel free to substitute a different squash or apple.

PENNSYLVANIA DUTCH CROOKNECK SQUASH AND BLACK TWIG APPLE SOUP

Serves 20-24

1 large crookneck squash

1/2 pound butter

6 Black Twig apples (cored, peeled and minced)

2 red onions, minced

8 cloves garlic, minced

2-3 carrots, minced

2 stalks celery, minced

1/2 gallon whole milk

1/2 gallon buttermilk

juice of one lemon

1 T cinnamon

1 1/2 tsp nutmeg

2 T fresh ginger, minced

Salt and fresh ground Black Pepper to taste

Bake squash until tender, about 1 1/2 hours at 350 degrees. Sauté apples and vegetables in the butter for 3-4 minutes. Remove squash from skin and add to pot. Sauté for another 3-4 minutes. Add whole milk, buttermilk, lemon juice and spices. Bring to almost a boil. Stir often! Puree with hand whisk or in blender. Serve piping hot.

LIVING LA DOLCE VITA WITH THE MCCAFFREY CLAN:

WELCOME TO MCCAFFREY'S DOLCE VITA, A COZY HIDEAWAY A STONE'S THROW OFF HIGHWAY 5

Tapestry Magazine November 2008

Is this heaven?
No -- it's Iowa.   *-- "Field of Dreams*

IN SEASON

By Jeff Severson

Jim McCaffrey's been reading my column.

That's the only way I can explain it. Did I not wax rhapsodic in these very pages just a few short months ago about how Lisa and I were attempting to capture la dolce vita (Italian for "the sweet life") at our own home in western Wisconsin? How we were trying to recreate our own little Italy, providing attitude adjustment via good food and wine and beautiful surroundings? Well, my fellow food columnist has just cut off a little slice for himself -- and I'm a little jealous.

It was a gorgeous Sunday, the bluffs bedecked in brilliant fall reds and golds, when we headed down the river to Lansing, IA, to meet Tapestry Magazine editorial director Julie Berg-Raymond and her husband, Bob. We continued west on

Highway 9 through 35 miles of bucolic Iowa farmland until we got to Decorah, heading north for just a couple of blocks on US Highway 52 before abruptly turning off and driving through a campground.

"Where are they taking us?," Lisa asked with a bit of skepticism. I thought of how many deadlines I'd missed, or had come close to missing, and wondered whether anyone would find our bodies back here. Suddenly, behind a pair of welcoming old apple trees, there it was. A beautiful new building in a Scandinavian/Northwoods style appropriate to the area, with a modest sign declaring, "McCaffrey's Dolce Vita." Off the

beaten path, but truly only a stone's throw (by C.C. Sabathia) off Highway 52.

Once inside, we were greeted warmly by the lovely Brenda McCaffrey, wife and soulmate of the chef and co-creator of this sunny and open, yet cozy, little hideaway. We were shown to a window booth with a cheery view of the apple trees and the deer that approach warily to avail themselves of the fallen fruit. The waiter arrived to take drink and appetizer orders, and we were officially on our way. Actually, the first thing we ordered was the soup of the day ($4 a cup/$6 a bowl) -- a seafood chowder that Lisa zeroed in on as soon as we walked in the door and saw it on the dry-erase board. (No one loves seafood like my Lisa.)

The soup plate arrived with a generous serving and four spoons so we could all share. I am not lying when I say this was probably one of the top five soups I've had in my life -- and that includes the baked French onion soup I enjoyed as a wide-eyed teenager with a glass of hearty red table wine in the stone-walled back room of a Paris bistro, accompanied by a Dylanesque guitar-playing troubadour singing French folk tunes. That's how good this soup is. The creation of Mike the head chef, this creamy classic is loaded with shrimp, crab and other seafood, a scandalous amount of butter and enough cream to make the Norwegian classic rømmegrøt. You may need an angioplasty afterwards, but it's worth it.

Wanting to get a good variety, we ordered three appetizers. I love an eclectic list representing various cuisines, and their short list does not disappoint. The Vietnamese spring rolls ($8) are impeccably fresh and much lighter than the deep-fried egg rolls we're all used to, with shrimp and Asian vegetables wrapped in wheat flour paper and served with a traditional hoisin-chili dipping sauce. The Italian-style stuffed mushrooms ($8), with sausage, garlic, Parmesan and other traditional ingredients, are some of the best I've had. Both of the recipes are in Jim's lighthearted yet very instructive and well-rounded book, Midwest CornFusion, and these two recipes alone are worth the price of admission.

But the third appetizer was the evidence that this rascal has been reading my column. My regular readers will recall a column in the spring or summer in which I described some excellent bacon-wrapped jalapeños we shared with friends and made at their wedding. Imagine my surprise when I saw Dolce Vita Poppers ($7) on the

menu: split jalapeños filled with cream cheese and wrapped with prosciutto. OK, so in true Italian fashion Jim uses prosciutto instead of the more pedestrian, greasy bacon. And maybe it's even a little better that way -- OK, maybe a lot. But remember, folks, you heard it here first. And it's not in his cookbook. Hmm...

I'd been waiting to meet Jim since he started writing for the magazine. When you read his column you just know he's someone you'd like -- a humble guy with a great sense of humor and serious food chops. In person he didn't disappoint. He was also in considerably better shape than yours truly, even though he's *a bit* older. Turns out he's lost twenty or so pounds since opening the place just a few weeks prior to our visit. (Note to self: Check into viability, considering current

market, of opening a little eatery.) Seriously, I'm not sure I could handle the ninety hours a week -- but it's obvious that Jim McCaffrey is passionate in the extreme about what he does. And for him it all starts with the pizza.

The restaurant is almost literally built around a pizza oven. Not just any pizza oven, but an honest-to-goodness European-style wood-fired oven built on site and equipped to produce a real Neapolitan-style pizza. And it is on this note that Jim McCaffrey borders on the fanatic. Many of his long hours are spent rolling out dough, which according to his standards must be almost paper-thin. The pizza, you see, is only in the oven for 90 seconds; the oven temperature is around 750 degrees -- 900 at the top. Now THAT's fast food. And real food.

We were famished, so we ordered three pizzas. The one I just had to have was the Margherita ($14), which many pizza aficionados consider the original pizza as enjoyed in Naples in the 1880s. Favored by and named for Queen Margherita of Savoy, this pizza represented the colors of the Italian flag with red tomato sauce, white mozzarella, and green basil. That's it -- and any serious pizzeria is to be judged on its most basic creation. (The only other pizza considered as seminal as a Margherita is the Naples original with nothing but cheese and anchovies.) Jim's Margherita did not disappoint; in fact, it was our favorite of the three. It is pizza in its naked, sublime form, showcasing the brilliance of the ingredients: thin sourdough crust, simple roasted garlic and herb tomato sauce, fresh cheese and garden-fresh basil. And according to Jim, it's the only thing he eats when he's hard at work at the restaurant. Speaking as one who could eat pizza literally every day, I'll have to say I can't blame him. This is la dolce vita at its finest.

The other two pizzas, as I figured, were also excellent. The shrimp pizza ($15) eschewed the usual tomato sauce for a garlic-infused olive oil covered with fresh mozzarella, shrimp, sliced Roma tomatoes, fresh basil and Parmesan. To me, the oil could have been a bit more garlic-infused, but I may have been jaded by the excellent Margherita -- and I have a really high garlic tolerance. The Thai Kickin' Chicken pizza ($16) featured a very authentic peanut sauce base topped with mozzarella, teriyaki-grilled lemon chicken, green onions, tomatoes and basil. I can only say "wow."

The menu also boasts sandwiches -- including New Orleans-style po' boys and a few entrees:

three Italian pasta dishes and a Cajun chicken Creole. So much good food, so little time. We did grab something to cleanse the palate, though: a Greek salad ($8) with fresh tomatoes, thinly sliced red onion, green pepper, kalamata olives and feta cheese, all tossed with a traditional lemon juice/olive oil dressing.

How about some dessert? After all that food, truthfully, we weren't much in the mood. But you can't really do a restaurant review without sampling a dessert, so we took one for the team and ordered the strawberry cheesecake. Cheesecake is all they offer, and it's actually not even on the menu; the server will let you know what's available that day. A local lady named Jane Bullerman makes such fabulous cheesecakes, Jim said, that he decided to offer them at the restaurant. It arrived with four forks so we could all sample it -- and it was fantastic. Dense, rich and beautifully marbled like an old-fashioned strawberry revel ice cream, it was the perfect ending to a terrific meal.

It's not often we drive more than an hour and a half for lunch. But I can honestly say I'd happily do it again. We absolutely loved the food, and more importantly, we enjoyed the hospitality. I felt like I had met a kindred spirit in Jim McCaffrey. He is a guy with whom I share more than newsprint. Jim has a real passion for food and for doing things his way (and it's not too different from how I would do it myself). We're all searching for our own version of la dolce vita. This guy has found it -- and he shares it with anyone who walks in the door.

Now that's always in season.

GUMBO: NOT JUST FOR BREAKFAST, ANYMORE

Tapestry Magazine December 2008

You know what the French say about British cooking: "If it's cold, it's soup, and if it's warm, it's beer." And the French certainly know their soup, especially bouillabaisse, the fish stew which is the base of the wonderful soup, gumbo.

Many French Acadians arrived and settled in Louisiana after being expelled by the British from Canada in 1755 and became known as Cajuns. They incorporated ingredients from the local Choctaw Indians (Sassafras leaves ground into a fine powder called file' powder) and okra which was brought to the area by West African slaves. Both were used as a thickener. Usually only one was used at a time, hardly ever together. A third thickener, roux, has been a more recent addition. This is usually made with lard or oil not butter. Because this roux is cooked until it gets a dark red (10 to 15 minutes), butter has a tendency to burn. If for some reason you do burn the roux, you need to throw it out and start anew.

Traditionally the holy trinity of vegetables (green peppers, onions, and celery) is added to the roux as it is cooking. This helps to cool the roux and sauté the vegetables as well. You then add stock, usually shellfish or chicken broth. Typically, a gumbo will have one or more kinds of poultry, smoked pork, and shellfish. Smoked pork might be Tasso ham or andouille sausage. If that is not available, you could substitute hot Italian sausage links. I just made a stock from shrimp tails and I am eagerly waiting to try making a gumbo with it.

You can do the same by peeling either cooked or uncooked shrimp. You can save up these shells in a ziplock bag in the freezer until you are ready to make stock. Just keep adding to the bag as you use more shrimp. When you are ready to make stock, put shells in a stockpot and cover with water by an inch or so. Add a little salt. Bring to a boil and simmer for 30-45 minutes.

This is so simple that even James Ronan could do it.

If there is just one Creole/Cajun dish you wish to master, this is probably the one. For American cuisine, gumbo is hailed as Louisiana's greatest culinary contribution. In 1885, The Creole Cookery Book called gumbo making an occult science that "should be allowed its proper place in the gastronomical world." So all of us Ragin' Cajun wannabes should take a walk on the wild side and pursue concocting a potful of this great American masterpiece.

All of us at McCaffrey's Dolce Vita would like to thank Julie for the wonderful coverage of our restaurant in last month's *Tapestry magazine*. We also would like to thank Jeff Severson for his review. You guys are great.

TRADITIONAL GUMBO

2 lbs shrimp (shelled and deveined)	1 large white onion, chopped
1 lb Andouille sausage, sliced	Salt to taste
10 cups shellfish or chicken broth	1 bunch green onions, chopped
1 lb cooked chicken breast, chunked	4 cups hot cooked rice
1/4 lb butter	2 celery stalks, chopped
1 tsp black pepper	1 1/2 cups chopped okra (fresh or frozen)
1 cup flour	1 tbl minced parsley
1 tbl Cajun seasoning	2 cloves garlic, minced

Add butter to a large pot. Melt. Add flour, stirring constantly, until it becomes a nutty brown or darker. Add veggies and cook stirring for five more minutes. Add broth and simmer for about π hour, stirring occasionally. Add shrimp, sausage and chicken breast and simmer until shrimp turns pink, about 2-3 minutes. Put a 1/2 cup of hot rice in a large soup bowl and ladle gumbo over it. Dig in!

TAPESTRY MAGAZINE 2009

CHILE AND THE MAN EPISODE NO. 1:
'THE CHARRO BEAN WAY'

Tapestry Magazine January 2009

In the summer and fall prior to erecting our restaurant building, we had quite a few gatherings on Sunday afternoons. The wood fired oven was stoked up awaiting crazy pizza fare to be inserted and extracted. We set up some tents to ward off potentially harmful rays from the god Sol for our fair-skinned Norwegian friends.

This accomplished, we began chopping, hacking, slicing, dicing, flailing, flagellating (whoops, strike that, there was no flagellation)

and generally making piles of tempting morsels of food to be consumed en masse throughout the afternoon. It was pure human vegamatic. No holds barred.

Any conceivable ingredient was always allowed and, in fact, heartily encouraged. One of my favorites was a pizza with garlic infused olive oil, thin slices of Yukon Gold potatoes, and topped with salt, fresh ground black pepper, and newly grated parmesan cheese. Another was olive-oil-marinated asparagus that been roasted on the grill with red onions and fresh tomato slices.

Yum! Kind of makes you think outside the box a little, doesn't it? (Wait until this spring, folks).

Whenever these gatherings occurred, an eclectic assortment of individuals would arrive bearing various pizza ingredients and, of course, beverages. On one particular occasion, the festivities were in full swing, pizzas were flying in and out of the oven at a furious pace, the Nordic women were looking good, as usual, and a good time was being had by all. This Irishman, in between trying to teach five year-olds the basics of Swiss yodeling, was attempting to explain to the Scandinavian male attendees that other cultures in the world do not put their food on colored plates in order to see what they are eating.

All of a sudden, the Mexican contingent arrived, brandishing bottles of tequila and yelling "We don't need no stinking tents!" What a wonderful addition to the festivities. Shanon's good friend,

Rob, has married Jeannette. And, it seems, when you marry a woman of Mexican descent, you become a member of a huge tight-knit community of family and friends. So a van-load of these family and friends pile out and join the fun games. After awhile, Jeannette's sister, Angel, gave me a present. A present like no other: A jar of homemade charro beans -- Mexican cowboy beans that is.

I opened. I tasted. I fell in love. Immediately I exclaimed "We must put these beans on a pizza!" Dough was rolled and brushed with olive oil. Next came beans, sliced fresh salt and peppered homegrown tomatoes and mozzarella cheese. Into to the oven, with its raging fire, it went. The wait, although only 90 seconds, seemed like an eternity. The result was incredible. The thin crust perfect, golden brown cheese, piping hot cilantro-laced beans, and fresh tomatoes. Ah, this was food for the gods.

I have thought about those beans for the last year and a half. I really didn't get to ask Angel how she made them. I see her rarely, as she lives up there in Minnesota. But as luck would have it, her ex-boyfriend (and father of their beautiful child, Lycia) helped us put up the restaurant towards the end. I guess he couldn't get enough of this Irishman.

So he stayed on as a cook when we opened up and has put up with me ever since. Enter Arnold Barrientos, Mexican, from Brownsville, Texas, and better known to his mother and friends as Chile. He's great. He's a dreamer just like me. Chile and the Man, we call ourselves. We even have a 19-step plan to become millionaires. (I'll let you know how that is going in future columns, ha ha). Anyway, we got to talking about how I really liked Angel's charro beans and decided to whip up a batch. We used them as a side dish over a weekend. Everyone loved them. I think they may go on our next menu.

So here is a gift from Chile and the Man, from an angel to me.

MEXICAN CHARRO BEANS

4 lbs dry pinto beans

32 cups water

4 peeled cloves garlic

1 large onion, peeled and quartered

One quarter cup salt

2 lbs bacon

2 large onions, diced

10 jalapeno peppers, de-stemmed, de-seeded, and minced

15 roma tomatoes, diced

1 oz. fresh cilantro, minced

Salt and fresh ground black pepper to taste

Spread beans out on a cookie sheet. Carefully sort out any dirt, rocks and broken beans and toss. In a large stockpot, cover beans with water by 5 or 6 inches. Soak overnight. Beans are ready when you can crush them between your fingers. Rinse beans. In a large clean stockpot, place beans, 32 cups water, garlic, onion, and one quarter cup salt. Bring to a boil and simmer for about an hour. Cut bacon into squares and fry in another large stockpot over medium heat. Do not drain. Add onions and cook until translucent. Add jalapeno peppers and cook another 3-4 minutes. Throw in beans. Add tomatoes and cilantro. Salt and pepper to taste. Enjoy.

WHAT A CUPID THING TO DO!
(OR THIS PHO IS FOR YOU, DEAR!)
Tapestry Magazine February 2009

Since Valentine's Day falls on a Saturday this year (that would be the 14th of February, guys) Brenda and I realized that we wouldn't be able to have our usual meal of romance on this occasion. We have an appointment with destiny at our restaurant, dishing up Dolce Vita delights for the lovebirds dropping that night. When I wrote my first Valentine's Day column a couple of years ago, I mentioned asking Brenda if she would like to work to put a romantic dinner together for the two of us. She replied, "Great, I'll pour the wine."

This year she graciously volunteered to pour again. She's such a trooper. I decided to make a dish that neither of us has had before. I recently read about a dish in Laos called Pho. It is a delicious noodle soup inspired by the national dish of Vietnam. The dish emerged from the country's having been colonized by the French, who introduced Pot au Feu (or, translated in English, Bowl of Fire. Whew!)

In my collection of cookbooks I could not find a single instance of Laotian cuisine cookery. I persevered, however, and came up with a book entitled "Quick and Easy Vietnamese Home Cooking for Everyone." On page 70, there is a recipe for Beef Pho. I scanned the list of ingredients and was dismayed. Egad! There was no fire in the recipe. Vowing to overcome this obstacle, I returned to the list and realized that a road trip would be necessary to acquire the proper ingredients.

Brenda agreed to accompany me on this journey to Rochester, MN -- to the Asian Food Store.

Accompanying us is "Quick and Easy Vietnamese Home Cooking for Everyone." I fully intended to make sure I came away with all the necessary knowledge and ingredients to construct this exotic soup. The lady clerk was extremely helpful. I asked her if she ever made Pho. She replied, "Of course." I then asked, "What about fire?" "Absolutely," she replied. "I use Sriracha Hot Chile Sauce." Eureka! Now we are talking.

I proceeded to the spice aisle, only to find that nary a spice has an English translation on it; they are all identified by Chinese symbols. Back to the clerk, to cajole her for help. Laughing, she leads this Irishman back to the aisle and we collect cinnamon sticks, anise stars, cloves, fish sauce and, finally, pho soup cubes. The recipe calls for one cube for four servings, but the clerk says she uses four cubes for six-eight servings -- Pho cubes: salt, sugar, monosodium glutamate and spices -- Hmm, the sacrifices I make for my column.

We gather our spices along with some fancy china teapots that Brenda wants for the restaurant. This accomplished, we head to Victoria's Italian restaurant. I highly recommend it. (In fact, we take my recommendation seriously enough to dine at Victoria's every couple of weeks.)

A couple of weeks later, we decide to celebrate Valentine's Day a little early. I head to our local meat department with my copy of "Quick and Easy Vietnamese Home cooking for Everyone," complete with pictures. I show Amy, butcher on duty, the picture of the soup with its thinly sliced beef and ask her what cut would work the best. We settle on the eye of the round. I gleefully drive home and begin to prepare for our special date. Of course I tweaked it a just little. But wow! Now I know why it is the national dish of Vietnam. So, here is my version.

Happy Valentine's Day from the both of us (and, Brenda, could I ask you to pour us another glass of wine? ...)

BEEF PHO

Garnish: Onion slices, cilantro, avocado slices

16 oz rice noodles

20 cups beef broth

1 lb fat trimmed beef eye of the round

2-3 cinnamon sticks

2 oz fresh ginger grated

6 whole anise stars

12 whole cloves

6 green onions

2 tbl butter

1/3 cup fish sauce

3 tbl sugar

2 tbl sriracha sauce

1 tbl salt

4 pho soup cubes (optional)

Cook in boiling water until tender. Drain and set aside. Combine all other ingredients and bring to a boil. Turn to a simmer. Cook beef to medium rare to medium. (about 5-6 minutes). Take out of stock and let cool. Slice across the grain very thinly. Strain broth. Divide noodles in bowls. Top with beef slices and garnish with onions, cilantro and avocado.

INSPIRED MAGAZINE COLUMNS
2009 - 2012

INTRODUCTION
INSPIRE(D) MAGAZINE

My last article for Tapestry Magazine was written for the final issue for February 2009. It was a sad period of time for all of us writers. It definitely left a huge void in my life. The creativity of putting together an article once a month had been extremely challenging but also greatly refreshing and rewarding. Because I was working sixty plus hours a week at my real job it sometimes was a hurdle to meet the Tapestry's deadlines. But I would not have had it any other way.

I took a little time off but soon the itch to get my creative juices flowing again was back. In September of 2007a local Decorah couple (newly weds at that) Benji and Aryn Nichols started a company called Inspire(d) Media. Along with several other venues, they began publishing Inspire(d) Magazine in October, 2007. It is a wonderful free magazine celebrating the good things in life and events in the Driftless Area. Once again this shanty Irish chef went with hat in hand to plead my case with Benji and Aryn to write my Mississippi Mirth columns for Inspire(d). We decided to try it once and see how it was accepted. My first article appeared in the October/November issue. Something must have worked because they still have my name listed in Inspire(d)'s credits. Thanks Benji and Aryn. You are great to work with.

INSPIRED MAGAZINE 2009

LIVE LIFE TO THE FULLEST
(A NATION OF COUCH POTATOES NO LONGER)

Inspired Magazine October/November 2009

If you are fortunate enough to live in Northeast Iowa as my wife, Brenda, and I do, then you have had the wonderful opportunity to experience the changing of seasons from summer into fall. An explosive collage of color descends upon the area as the flora metamorphoses from the greens of the past six months into its final hurrah before the harsh reality of winter arrives. Brilliant shades of red, orange, and yellow merge into a kaleidoscope of panoramic splendor. Nature provides a unique setting of which one should take full advantage. So instead of being a horizontal couch slouch, unglue your hand from the remote, and spend a little quality time with your loved ones in the great outdoors. Leave the drone of ESPN behind, participate in one or all of the following activities, have some darn good fun, and then, we'll do lunch.

The old saying, "The best things in life are free" is certainly applicable to Decorah and the surrounding area. There are miles of trails in its great parks. Hiking one of these numerous paths can be an exhilarating experience. It is also great exercise. Be sure to wear good shoes. High heels and flip flops can be disasters in the waiting; there are lots of ups and downs. A few years back, Brenda and I traversed these trails extensively as we trained to hike in and out of the Grand Canyon in one day. Ok, we were idiots, but our training trails definitely built the leg muscles we needed to accomplish that feat. The added bonus of hiking is just to be out in the woods enjoying nature. Breathe it all in. For me, a heightened awareness of my surroundings occurs when I'm out of my normal environment an in someone or something else's. The solitude of the woods accompanied by the occasional bird twitter, a couple of squirrels chasing each other, a bright leaf or two falling, or a pair of red tailed hawks in search of a tasty mouse for their noon meal certainly tunes into one's mind that we are just a miniscule drop in the pool of life. Actually, kind of humbling when you sit down and think about it.

Another great but lesser utilized outdoor activity readily available in Northeast Iowa is fossil hunting. The entire family can, pretty much, participate. My grandsons, who are five and six, just love to go. They have a big advantage over grandpa. Hey, they are short, sharp eyed, and quick to the find. Ah, youth! I started out as a child myself. The innocence and wonder of discovery still remains with me. Well, maybe not the innocence. Ok, I digress. Dry creek beds full of broken limestone are an ideal place to get started. Bring some sacks along to put your millions-of-years-old treasures in and wear "GOOD SHOES." Move slowly scanning the rocks at your feet. Not only will you find fossils but lots of other interesting items. The last time

I went was with my grandson, August. His bag contained some pretty important stuff. A few fossils, some pretty rocks, a lot of acorns, several abandoned snail shells, and a couple of fuzzy caterpillars to take home to mom and dad to put in jars with grass for the winter. Butterflies in the making. That plan was quashed, however, when we returned home only to find the crafty little rascals had made their escape. Other great places to find fossils are the sand and rock bars aligning both sides of the Upper Iowa River. With each new flood these rocks are turned over revealing a host of new finds. These areas are also great places to teach the young ones the art of skipping stones. Knowledge like this is always extremely handy.

My last favorite fall activity is hunting late-season mushrooms. This, of course, can be incorporated into the previous two forays. It can be a little dicey as well, so if you are not sure of a mushroom's edibility, ask someone who does or just throw it away to avoid any problems. One of the easiest fall mushrooms to identify are giant puffballs. They are found growing on the ground in meadows and forests. They are round and I have found ones the size of a basketball that weighed up to 25 pounds. Make sure you only pick ones that look freshly white and are solid throughout when cut open. They have a wonderful earthy flavor. Cut them into steaks and sauté in butter and minced garlic. Heaven! Chicken in the Woods is another great fall mushroom in this area. You can find them mostly growing on dying or dead oak trees. They will be growing on the side of the tree about three feet up or so. They are bright yellow with maybe a little orange. They can get pretty large as well. 15 to 20 pounds is not unusual. Do not rip them off of the tree. Just cut close to the bark so it grows again the next year. A third option is found on Box Elder trees. These mushrooms grow in knotholes or tree injuries. They are known as elm mushrooms. Very edible and delightful. They look like common white field mushrooms and are a little milder. Sometimes they are higher up than you can reach, so you can work on your tree climbing skills as well.

As long as you are out and about separated from the idiot box, you might want to check the local farmers' market too. Pick up some great fresh produce, use it in the following recipe, and grab a loaf of newly baked bread to accompany the meal as well. Whew! All this exercise has worn me out. I wonder if the Hawkeye game is being televised.

MUSHROOM TURKEY KABOBS

2 lbs. fall mushrooms
2 garlic cloves, minced
2 lbs. boneless turkey breast
1 T. sesame seed oil
4 T. Worcestershire sauce
1 cup orange juice

6 T. balsamic vinegar
2 large onions, cut into 1/8's
1 cup extra virgin olive oil
3 green peppers, cut 1"X1"
3 T. minced fresh chives ½ lb. cherry
  tomatoes

Cut mushrooms and turkey into bite sized pieces. In a large bowl mix Worcestershire, balsamic vinegar, olive oil, chives, garlic, sesame seed oil, and orange juice for a marinade. Add mushrooms and turkey. Cover and chill 2-3 hours. Preheat BBQ grill. Have 12 metal or presoaked wooden skewers on hand. Thread with a piece of mushroom, turkey, onion, green pepper, and tomato. Twice for each skewer. Grill, turning skewers often, until turkey is cooked completely through. Serve with Darlene's rice.

DARLENE'S RICE

3 cups chicken broth
½ tsp. turmeric
1 ½ cups rice

1 ½ T. soy sauce
½ tsp curry powder
1/2 cup golden raisins

Mix all dry ingredients in a large heavy duty pot. Add broth. Bring to a boil. Cover with tight fitting lid. Simmer for 20 minutes. Serve it up! Delicious!

REACH OUT A HAND
(GIVE A LIFT TO YOUR FELLOW MAN.)

Inspired Magazine December 2009/Januray 2010

I got to thinking about what inspires volunteerism recently. It was after McCaffrey's Dolce Vita joined several other area restaurants in hosting groups for Decorah's Holiday Showcase of Homes Tour.

Two stellar volunteers, Linda Quaas and Kris Kraft, formulated this novel idea just two short years ago. They approached the Winneshiek Medical Center Foundation. A committee would be formed. It would solicit four homeowners to open their doors and let area merchants deck their homes out for the holidays with products from their stores. It was a lot of work for the committee, merchants and staff, and the homeowners too. Applause! Applause! This year's event raised funds for Winneshiek Medical Center to purchase two new Advanced Life Support monitors for its ambulances. It was a rousing success, raising $28,000 for the project. The Dolce Vita had the breakfast buses. We served fresh spinach and onion quiche, popovers, and fresh fruit salad along with mimosas. Nothing like a little champagne for breakfast to whet one's enthusiasm for the upcoming day!

When the buses pulled up at 7:30 am, it was still pretty dark out. A bevy of excited ladies, along with a sprinkling of men, descended upon us. While our staff and some volunteers were getting food and drinks out to everyone, three more tour volunteers were arranging raffle ticket sales. $5 a ticket with a chance to win half the pot as prizes during the meal. The other half went to support the event. One volunteer, the ever so elegant Elea Uhl, enthusiastically exhorted her captive audience of the enchanting prospect of extra enrichment for the holidays. (How do you like that line, eh?) Everybody reached for their purse or wallet. Amazingly well organized and efficient. I was duly impressed. After a culmination of ten months of hard work and dedication, the end result was truly outstanding. A commitment of many to achieve a common goal. This was true altruism.

A few days after, I thought about this project and others. I pondered the motivation. Is it an act of selfishness to be rewarded by someone's smile and gratitude or truly an act of selflessness? Probably the line falls somewhere in the middle. Definitely nothing to feel guilty about, however. Volunteerism is a gift of the most precious possession a person has. The gift of time. As poet/songwriter James Durst said, "Help one another; there is no time like the present and no present like time." Material goods come and go but the memory of lending a hand to a friend, stranger, or community is for a lifetime. Besides that, it just feels good, gol' darn it! As I go through life, sometimes I just shake my head and chuckle. The paradox is this: I find as a rule the busiest people I know are also the ones I see doing the greatest amount of community service. Those type A people just never seem to be able to sit down.

One of my favorite projects that I have been fortunate enough to be involved in is "Empty Bowls." This event raises funds for local food pantries or national projects like Lutheran World Relief. Restaurants, bakeries and private individuals make soup and bread, and area potters throw one-of-a-kind soup bowls. For a donation of $20, a person selects a bowl and has a choice of a multitude of different soups and bread. They take the bowl home as a remembrance of the event. There is electricity in the air. Everybody is abuzz. All of the many volunteers and attendees are overtly enthusiastic. It is a win-win situation for everyone. Last year more than 900 people shared the communal tables at Empty Bowls. A time to make new friends and renew relationships with old friends. I was in charge of soup. (Who made that decision?). We had something like 180 gallons with very little left at the end. This type of project is so inspiring. You just want to be involved.

Now that the holiday season is descending upon us, take a moment or two to reflect on the real meaning of giving. There always is someone who is less fortunate than ourselves. Whether we help individually or as a community, we become a stronger society because of it. Lily Tomlin once said "Somebody should do something about that. Then I realized I was a somebody." Be that somebody and reach out. It just feels good!

If you are thinking of volunteering, here are a few places to take a look at in the area: Northland Agency on Aging which provides Meals on Wheels to inbound citizens and other services, any of the area nursing homes, Winneshiek Medical Center, Seed Savers Exchange, public libraries, RSVP (Retired Senior Volunteer Program) which is located in the Decorah Public Library, local museums and schools just to name a few.

SPINACH AND ONION QUICHE

1 9-inch deep dish pie crust
1 egg yolk beaten

Filling
1 pkg fresh spinach
1 red onion sliced
1 ½ cups grated Swiss cheese
1 cup heavy cream
3 eggs beaten
1/8 tsp ground nutmeg
½ tsp salt
¼ tsp white or black pepper

Preheat the oven to 375 degrees. Brush pie crust with beaten egg yolk. Cover the bottom of the crust with spinach. Add a layer of onion. Cover with half of the cheese. Add another layer of spinach and onion. (You will have enough left over for the start of a salad.) Cover with the other half of the cheese. Whisk the remaining ingredients together and pour over the top of the pie. Bake for 30 to 40 minutes until a toothpick inserted in the center comes clean.

(Author's note: This is for all of the ladies on the bus tour who asked for the quiche recipe.)

INSPIRED MAGAZINE 2010

A STELLAR STELLA
(WELCOME TO A NEW BEGINNING)

Inspired Magazine February/March 2010

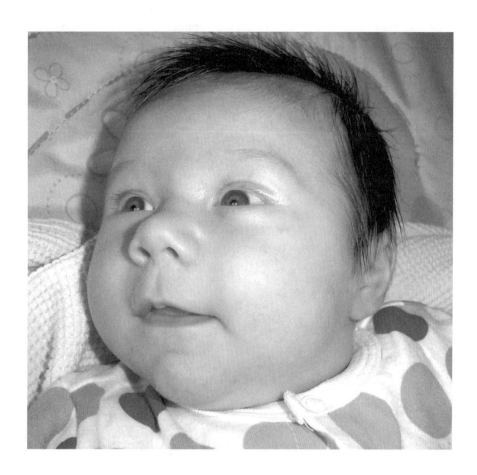

On November 9, 2009, a small but shining star entered our world for the first time. Stella Marie Witt was born a month early at 5 pounds 15 ounces with a head of black hair to match even that of her grandmother Brenda. Feisty, and a Scorpio, again like her grandmother. Her parents, Craig and Fawn Witt, were thrilled to have her arrive as healthy as a newborn premie can be. As soon as she was bundled up, she was more than ready to get on with one of life's greatest pleasures: gastronomy. Since her mother had to go to the ICU, it was just a bottle of formula, but one has to begin somewhere. It looks like she is off to a great start as she has weighed in at almost twice her birth weight at two months. Ah, to be young again. Eat, burp, look around at new surroundings, pass gas, and sleep....

I am in the process of writing a new book that is, in part, a cookbook. I thought it would be fitting if this grandfather came up with a recipe that was dedicated to this delightful child. (No grandparental pride here, eh?) It will be years before she will truly enjoy this dish but at least she will know that her grandfather was thinking of her. I pondered for a while on a creation. There really is no such animal as a new recipe, only variations on old ones. So I started with something everybody loves: pancakes. And not just any pancakes, mind you, French pancakes.

More commonly known as crepes, these thin little treats are perfect to wrap around savory or sweet tidbits. They originally hailed from Brittany, France, but are now common throughout the entire country and have gained world renown. Crepes are simple to make and can be the base structure for many a delectable culinary experience. Heat a 7-inch fry pan (stick or non-stick) to medium high heat. Add a little cooking oil, butter, or cooking spray to the pan. Take off the heat. Pour in one-quarter cup of crepe batter (recipe follows). Tilt the pan from side to side until it is entirely covered with batter. Return to the heat. Cook until the edges start to brown and the interior begins to solidify (about a minute). Using a small plastic spatula, gently slide under the crepe and flip it over. Continue cooking for another 20-30 seconds to brown the second side. Slide off onto a plate. Repeat the process and stack on top of each other until you have made enough for your project. If the crepes stick to the pan, you probably do not have your pan hot enough. It needs to heat up evenly all across the cooking surface. Usually, two stuffed crepes are sufficient for an entrée.

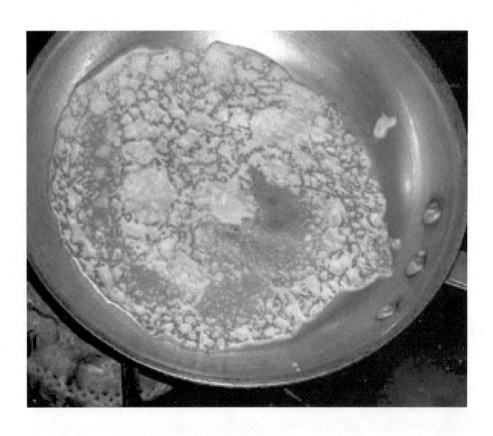

OK! We have all mastered the art of cooking French Crepes 101. So let the fun begin. What shall we stuff these little darlings with? Since Stella is a new arrival, I decided to start with one of spring's new arrivals as well. Young and tender skinny shoots of asparagus immediately came to mind. Definitely in the top 10 of my favorite vegetables to eat. I thought that a little color contrast and the tart sweetness of a sliced red onion would complement the asparagus very nicely. And one theory of life is that everything started from the sea. So, I added some shrimp to

boot. After sautéing Stellar Stella's Savory Crepe ingredients, it was time to assemble. First preheat the oven to 325 degrees. Then take three shoots of asparagus and place on the bottom third of the crepe. Top with some sautéed red onion. Place three shrimp in a row over the asparagus and onion. Roll up crepe starting the bottom side and place seam side down in a baking dish. Repeat the process until all of the crepes are made. Sprinkle with Swiss cheese. You will want to warm these up, but you do not want to overcook (just 15 – 20 minutes). While the crepes are basking in the heat of the oven, take this time to whip up some Hollandaise sauce (Recipe follows). This can be a little tricky. I find it easier to have someone help out by pouring the melted butter in while I hold the pan with the egg mixture in one hand and constantly whisk that mixture with the other hand.

It is time to plate up. Take the baking dishes out of the oven. Use a spatula and scoop out two crepes per person and place just off center on a plate. Drizzle with Hollandaise sauce. Put a couple sprigs of parsley on top and add two or three slices of fresh tomato on the side. Bon Appetite! Whew, this has been a lot of work! Time to join Stella and eat, burp, look around, pass gas, and sleep. Ciao!

CREPES

Makes 8 servings (16 crepes)

Crepe Batter

2 large eggs
1 cup milk
1/3 cup water

1 cup all purpose white flour
¼ tsp salt
2 Tbl melted butter

Whisk eggs in a mixing bowl until frothy. Blend in milk and water. Add flour and salt. Whisk or stir until batter is smooth. Stir in melted butter. Refrigerate for 2 hours. Follow French Crepes 101 above for cooking instructions.

Crepe Filling

48 asparagus shoots

1 red onion peeled, halved, and sliced thin

48 large shrimp, peeled and deveined (31-40 count for size)

Three cloves garlic, minced fine

Extra virgin olive oil for sautéing

1/2 lb grated Swiss cheese to sprinkle over filled crepes

Sliced tomato and parsley for garnish

Sauté asparagus and onion in olive oil with salt and pepper for about three minutes until the onion is translucent and the asparagus is bright green and just softened. Sautee shrimp until just pink – about three minutes – in olive oil with fresh garlic. (Don't overcook – they will turn rubbery and tough).

HOLLANDAISE SAUCE

2 ½ sticks butter, melted
6 large egg yolks
2 tsp lemon juice

Dash of cayenne pepper
Salt and white pepper to taste

In a bowl or top of a double boiler whisk eggs until frothy.
Place over a small pot or bottom of double boiler with barely boiling water. Continue to whisk until eggs start to thicken, about three minutes. Remove from heat and slowly whisk in warm melted butter. Whisk in lemon juice and salt and peppers.

Assemble (steps above), plate and drizzle with Hollandaise sauce. Add sliced tomatoes and parsley for garnish. Serve immediately.

CINCO DE MAYO
(A CELEBRATION FOR ALL)

Inspired Magazine April/May 2010

My brother, Pete, loves a good party. Especially on May 5th, his birthday. Coincidentally, it's also the date of the Mexican holiday Cinco De Mayo. Primarily a regional holiday in the Mexican state of Puebla, it celebrates the unlikely 1862 victory of an under-armed Mexican militia of just 4000 troops over a French army that was double its size and vastly more equipped. Significant for the United States, the defeat stopped Napoleon III from supplying arms and money to Confederate rebels engaged in the Civil War against the Union Army. That helped the Union defeat the Confederates in the Battle of Gettysburg.

Worldwide, Cinco De Mayo has become a celebration of Mexican heritage and pride. Beyond the flamenco dancing and mariachi bands, it is a wonderful opportunity to experience local cuisines from different regions of our southern neighbors. Brenda and I have been fortunate enough to have traveled to Mexico several times. Our first trip was to

Mazatlan on the Pacific coast. We stayed at the Riviera Beach Resort otherwise known as "Party Central." An ice-cold bucket of beers (8) was $6. Every other hour was Happy Hour and you got TWO buckets of beer for $6. No extra charge for slices of lime. Having not studied Spanish, we felt that it was of immediate importance to immerse ourselves in the language. Hector Cortez, the head bartender, graciously accepted the role of teacher. The two phrases of greatest significance he taught us were, "Dos cervesas, por favor" (Two beers, please) and "Donde este el bano?" (Where is the bathroom?). A wise man, that Hector.

All joking aside, Brenda and I have found the people we met in Mexico to be warm, gracious, and very giving. Family and friends always seem to be at the core of life there. When a party happens, everyone is invited. Aunts and uncles, matriarchs and patriarchs, siblings, nieces and nephews, etc., etc., etc. People dress up in their Sunday best to pay respect to the family putting on the extravaganza. Food is always the star attraction, shared by one and all. I think one of the reasons that Cinco De Mayo is so popular in the United States is that it affords Mexican immigrants and descendants an opportunity to remember and carry on their family cultural heritage. And lucky for all the rest of us, we can participate too.

Since Napoleon III and future French attempts failed to colonize Mexico and turn the Gulf of Mexico into The New World French Riviera complete with little bistros serving baguettes and lattes, Spanish and Portuguese influences on local cuisine were more predominant. One of these influences was the introduction of limes in the mid 1600s. Limes could be used for many purposes but one of the most significant was the ability to pickle fresh fish and other seafood with their acidic juices. A combination of lime juice and local indigenous ingredients such as chiles, tomatoes and avocado produced the Mexican version of ceviche. Ceviche is a wonderful appetizer served up and down both coasts of Mexico as well as Central and South America. I like to serve it in footed sundae glasses accompanied by tortilla chips. Throw in a few Corona or Dos Equis beers complete with wedges of lime and you will have a great beginning for a Cinco De Mayo party of your own. And don't forget to invite my brother, Pete.

The daily bread of Mexican cuisine is the tortilla. It has provided sustenance for hundreds of years. Actually, evidence has been produced that a basic version of the tortilla dated back to 10,000 B.C. The versatility of the tortilla is seemingly endless. It is the backbone for tacos, tostadas, burritos, enchiladas, quesadillas, and more. The primary ingredient is corn but in Northern Mexico wheat has been introduced as an alternative ingredient. The age-old dilemma of what to do with leftover bread, in this instance, tortillas, exists in Mexico also. In French cuisine, day-old crusty baguettes are sliced, put in a rich hot sautéed onion beef broth, and covered with gruyere cheese that is then placed under a broiler. French Onion soup becomes a fantastic venue for leftover bread. Lesser known – but equally fantastic – is Mexico's favorite son, Tortilla Soup. When Brenda and I stayed at the Riviera Beach Resort for the first time, we found it necessary after a couple hours of "Happy Hour" festivities to head over to the resort restaurant, El Ancla. Proper nourishment was in order. Brenda chose soup and salad, her custom request. I opted for chicken fajitas. When our food came, Brenda had a spoonful of her soup and said, "Jim, you have to try this." I did. I felt I had just grabbed the brass ring on the merry-go-round at the county fair. It was Tortilla Soup and the taste was out of this world. I had to have the recipe. I asked our waiter if I could speak to the chef. "Si, Si." The head chef, Ignacio, came out. He could speak about as much English as I could speak Spanish. I eventually went out and corralled Hector, who was able to convey my request. A couple of days later, when we went down for breakfast, Ignacio slipped me a piece of paper handwritten in Spanish. The Holy Grail of soup. It took me a couple of years to get it translated correctly but it is certainly worthy to adorn your Cinco De Mayo table.

Hasta la vista! Time for me to round up a few Coronas and a Mariachi band for Pete's birthday. Anybody know any flamenco dancers? Have a great Cinco De Mayo!

SEAFOOD CEVICHE

8 oz. precooked shrimp, peeled and deveined

1 small red onion, sliced thin

2 ripe avocados

8 oz. bay scallops

2 tsp. Mexican oregano

8 oz. fresh or thawed haddock or cod cut in ½ inch cubes

Salt

Fresh ground black pepper

10-12 limes

Fresh parsley or cilantro sprigs

4 Roma tomatoes, diced

Tortilla chips

In a 9 x 13 non-metallic baking dish, combine seafood, tomatoes and onion. Cover completely with lime juice. Cover and refrigerate for about 4 hours. Drain. Place in large bowl. Cut avocados in half lengthwise. Twist sides and remove pit. Scoop out avocado meat and dice into ½ inch pieces. Add with oregano to seafood mixture.

Salt and pepper to taste. Plate up, garnish with sprigs and pass the tortilla chips. Serves 6.

IGNACIO'S TORTILLA SOUP

3 T olive oil

32 oz chicken broth

2 garlic cloves, minced

white pepper

1 medium onion, diced fine

1 can evaporated milk

1 tsp Mexican oregano

1 lb shredded Chihuahua cheese

1oz.fresh basil, shredded small

1- 28 oz tomato sauce (fresh or canned)

2 avocados, peeled and sliced

24 tortilla chips

Saute garlic and onion until translucent, 2-3 minutes. Add chicken broth, tomato sauce, oregano, basil and white pepper to taste. Simmer twenty minutes. Place 3 tortilla chips in the bottom of a soup bowl. Add some milk and cheese. Pour soup over top. Garnish with avocado. Serves 8.

FATHERHOOD, FATHER'S DAY, AND FRESH OFF OF THE GRILL

Inspired Magazine June/July 2010

I became a father by blood on September 7, 1980. Our son, Conor, was delivered by c-section after an epic 12-hour struggle to stop Brenda's contractions. He was 45 days premature and weighed in at a whopping three pounds 14 ounces. Brenda came home after a week, but due to complications, Conor remained with the wonderful staff at Gundersen Lutheran Hospital in La Crosse, Wisconsin, for six-plus weeks. He was a fighter. Twice we were called to the hospital because they didn't think he was going to make it. They even had to place a shunt in his head to drain fluid that was placing pressure on his brain. But as soon as he came out of surgery our little tiger pulled the breathing tubes out of his nose and never looked back. When we finally were able to bring him home, he weighed just a little over five pounds. In an ironic twist of life, he grew to be one of the tallest in his class.

Prior to Conor's arrival, I was a father by virtue of marriage. Brenda's other two children, Shanon and Fawn – through no fault of their of their own, – became destined to be raised by an Irish guy who didn't have a clue about what being a father was all about. Poor kids. The lessons of fatherhood were thrust upon me like a bolt of summer lightning. I wisely decided early on that whatever Brenda told her children, I would back 100 percent. So when she grounded one of them for the rest of their life, I would agree and say, "Yep, you are grounded for the rest of your life." A half an hour later, Brenda would relent and the rules would change. I would then ask if she thought this might confuse the children. It certainly was confusing me. I was raised that Dad's word was final and no amount of cajoling would change it.

My father grew up on a farm near the (Iowa) Twin Cities – Burr Oak and Bluffton. His mother died at an early age. His father liked to spend a few hours in the tavern after chores, so Dad and his father would hitch up their team of horses and head to town. (Er, village). Dad would usually hang out with the horses until it was time to go home. I think things were tough for him. He walked to a one-room country school a mile every day even in rain, snow, or freezing temperatures – "uphill both ways," of course. During the Great Depression, he and his father burned field corn for heat because prices were so low they couldn't afford to haul it to market. He picked potatoes in Idaho with a couple of his buddies one summer too. They would wrap potatoes in aluminum foil and drop them into the wide mouthed radiator of their tractor. It was about all they had to eat. So he grew up tough. He had to in order to survive.

Thus it was with tough love that Dad raised his five children. He worked hard and put in long hours. He taught us the value of hard work, honesty and integrity. He taught us how to garden. When we had a bit of free time, he taught us how to fish. But he did not teach us how to hug or say "I love you." I think that came from his single parent childhood. He was never awarded that type of affection. But he was a good father and all of the grandchildren – including Shanon and Fawn – loved him. I brought this tough love upbringing into my family. Brenda brought the hugs and "I love yous". Somehow everything meshed. I became a father with a different view of raising family than my father. We have become a very tight and close-knit family. We have to be. Brenda and I, Shanon, Fawn, and Conor are all owners and partners in our restaurant, McCaffrey's Dolce Vita. We work together side-by-side every day, and as with any business, we don't always see eye-to-eye.

But there haven't been any fistfights yet.

Usually at the end of the day, we are still hugging and saying I love you. I guess that fatherhood thing panned out.

We now have a couple more fathers in our growing family. Shanon is 6-year-old Kamran's father. Craig, who is married to Fawn, is the father of their two children: 6-year-old August and 6-month-old Stella.

Since we're open for business on Father's Day, I plan on inviting all the fathers and the rest of the family over the Monday after for a belated celebration. I shall do as nature intended a father to do: barbeque. I am going south of the border with the menu, making a little Mexican street vendor food. Accompanying the usual homemade salsa, guacamole, and chips, I'm grilling "roadside chicken" with green onions. The following method is an adaptation of a Rick Bayless recipe. And sweet corn should be in season! In Mexico, I found sweet corn grilled on the barbeque to be almost heaven. Grilling accomplished, I probably will crack open some ice-cold cervezas and propose a toast to Dad, fathers, and fatherhood. Then I think I'll take a nap. Because that's what being a father is all about.

GRILLED ROADSIDE CHICKEN

(serves four)

1 3 lb chicken (cut into 8 pcs)	¼ tsp cinnamon
2 bunches green onions	2 cloves garlic, minced
1 ½ tsp ancho chile powder	3 T apple cider vinegar
1 teaspoon Mexican oregano	¼ cup orange juice
¼ tsp ground cloves	1 tsp salt

Wash chicken with cold water and pat dry with paper towels. Place in a 9x13 baking dish. Trim green onions of any wilted leaves and roots. Set aside. Combine remaining ingredients to make a marinade. Coat all sides of the chicken with marinade. Let rest for 30 minutes. The chicken should be grilled over indirect heat. If using a gas grill, light the outside burners and leave the center one off. With a charcoal grill, push the grill ready coals to one side. You will have to add more coals about half way through.

Place chicken on the non-heated portion of the grill. Cook without turning. Baste occasionally with remaining marinade. Chicken is ready when juices run clear. (about 45 minutes). About 10 minutes before chicken is ready brush green onions with vegetable or olive and place over direct heat until tender. Place chicken on cutting board for and cover with foil for 10 minutes. Serve two pieces per person with grilled onions on top.

GRILLED SWEET CORN WITH LIME BUTTER

4 Large ears sweet corn	¼ tsp cayenne pepper
1 stick butter	Salt and fresh ground black pepper
2 limes	

Remove husks and silk from sweet corn. Bring grill up to high heat. Place corn on grill and turn frequently. When corn has a nice char all the way around it is good to go. Melt butter. Cut limes in half. Squeeze juice into melted butter. Add cayenne pepper and stir.

Baste corn with lime butter. Salt and pepper to taste. Ole!!

IRISH INGENUITY? OR JUNKYARD DOG?
DOG? YOU BE THE JUDGE.

Inspired Magazine August/September 2010

So what does a 220-gallon oil tank rescued from your dad's salvage yard, a Rambler front-end chassis complete with chrome hubcaps with embossed red letter 'R's, and an dilapidated old boat trailer have in common?

Stick around. There's a story to be told here. One night after closing last winter, I was sitting at our restaurant bar with Dolce Vita head chef, Mike Domine (aka Mike D.). While sipping on a couple of cold ones, we were discussing the batch of ribs he had made that night and how they could improve.

"You know, we really ought to have a smoker," Mike D. comments.

Now there was food for thought. I dwelled upon that for about three seconds, took a sip of Pinot Grigio, and replied, "Yeah, that sure would be super. Adding some smoke to those ribs would definitely put them in a class of their own. However, you know as well as I, that Brenda (my lovely wife and the woman who cooks the books for our company) – with the current state of the economy – is no way going to let us take 10 or 15 Gs to purchase one of those mammoth boy toys. Mike D. replies, "Yeah… but it still would be nice."

In the early 1980s, when Brenda and I had the Café Deluxe in Downtown Decorah, our friend and local welding shop entrepreneur, John Beard, built us a stationary barbeque for the outside dining patio. It, basically, was an old oil tank pulled from someone's basement when they switched to gas for their primary heat source. John cut the tank in half the long way, reinforced the edges with angle iron, and hinged the two pieces. We went to Carlson Construction, a cement and sand company, and purchased a couple of discarded shaker grates. John incorporated these into a platform on the bottom to hold charcoal or wood and a cooking surface. Pretty much everything in the cooker was recycled. Hey, 30 years ago, we were going green and didn't even know it!

At the first Nordic Fest we used the cooker, we served barbeque chicken with homemade potato salad and fresh sweet corn. We had people lined up for two blocks after the parade. 400 servings in two hours. Now that was a lot of cluckers.

A few years later, Brenda and I sold the Café. The cooker went along in that transaction. But I had the itch. Barbeque was in the blood. Bigger was better. Visions of grilling for the masses was occurring in my head. My kingdom for a BBQ.

One day, after work, I stopped up to see my dad at his salvage yard. Low and behold, there was another oil tank standing out front. That got the adrenaline pumping. "So Dad, what are you going to do with that?" I query. "They are a real pain," he replies. "By the time and gas you spend cutting them up you end up losing money." "Do you want me to take it off your hands?" I ask. "It will only cost you a beer." A split six-pack later the deal was consummated. Since John was busy with a large project, I got my brother Pat (welder extraordinaire as well) involved. I wanted this unit to be mobile. Pat pulled the front-end chassis off of an old Rambler from the salvage yard. After modifying it to fit under the tank, he cut the tongue off of an old boat trailer and mounted it to the chassis. A couple more shaker grates and we were ready to rock and roll.

I spent a weekend burning wood on the inside to get rid of any potential oil residue. Then the project got put on hold. I started working at the Calmar Manufacturing Company. I also started building a house. So the rig sat for 25 years.

Back at the bar I say to Mike D., "You know, I think I may have a solution to this little problem. I have that old barbeque cooker down on the bottom that we could modify into a smoker. It will have to wait until spring as it is only buried under 24 feet of snow." Mike D. replies, "Yeah, that sure would be nice."

Spring arrived. When the ground dried out, I had Conor, my son, pull the rig out with his pickup. Completely rust-covered, tires rotten, and a missing bottom shaker grate. But other than that, she was cherry. Pat was busy working on his new place and John, our newly-elected state representative, was in Des Moines legislating. So I called a third area welder/fabricator/friend, Jan Dansdill, to see if he had time to work on our little project.

In the meantime, one of our friends came by to take a look. He had two good used tires in his garage that would fit and he would be willing to donate. Conor pulled the wheels off. When Jan showed up, we were road ready. I explained that besides being a barbeque rig, we wanted to use it as a smoker. We needed to cut holes on the backside and construct a smoker box. Three days later, after some other modifications and a new paint job, Jan pulled it into the parking lot. He added a couple of wings on the side to hold food and utensils, a new handle made out of heavy-duty truck exhaust pipe, and a chimney with an enclosed damper. A Cadillac of a rig.

Well, almost. Jan left. Brenda to come down to take a look, and after explaining the different details, I went into the building to close up. When I came out, the cooker was partially turned over and Brenda was down for the count.

She had decided to shut the hood and it tipped over on her. Good thing these Bowegians have hard noggins, 'cause she escaped with just a bump on her head. We added some stabilizer legs and it was finally done. 1,566 square inches of cooking area. Room for 300 hot dogs. One heck of a weenie roast. Smoker works great as well. It has only been 25 years in the works, but as an old buddy of mine used to say, "It isn't a record." And for 99 percent of you testosterone laden, bbq-crazed, alpha males, I've just one thing to say: "Mine's bigger......er..... my Smoker, that is

SMOKED BBQ CHICKEN QUARTERS

(serves eight)

8 chicken quarters w/skin on

Rub

½ cup no salt garlic and herb seasoning

2 tsp cayenne pepper

2 tsp paprika

Sauce

1 cup Open Pit BBQ Sauce

1 cup Pace Medium Picante Sauce

Juice of one lemon

2 garlic cloves minced

Soak wood chips (hickory, cherry, pecan, apple) in water 2 hours prior to start. Preheat oven at 500 degrees. Rinse chicken off with cold running water. Discard any excess fat. Pat dry with paper towels. Wash hands with soap and hot water. Arrange chicken skin side up in a single layer in a couple 11 x 19 shallow baking dishes. Mix rub ingredients. Generously sprinkle rub mixture on chicken pieces. Gently massage rub into the skin. Place dishes into the oven for eight minutes. This will sear the juices in. Reduce heat to 350 degrees. Bake uncovered for another 30 minutes or so. Usually when the juices run clear, the chicken is cooked thoroughly. It is best to check with a meat thermometer. Insert in the deep part of the thigh. It needs to read 165 degrees minimum. While chicken is baking, prepare outside grill for smoking. If using charcoal, stack briquettes to one side and light. With gas, light a burner on one side. When grill is hot, place wood chips in a small metal pie tin and place directly over heat. When wood chips start smoking, arrange chicken on grill away from the heat. Cover. Let smoke for 15 to 20 minutes. Meanwhile, mix sauce ingredients. Baste chicken liberally with sauce. Cover again for 10 to 15 minutes. Baste once more and repeat. Time to eat. This is a fast way to get the smoked flavor. One can also just put the chicken on the grill in the same fashion and cook and smoke it from the beginning. This will probably take 3 to 4 hours. Remember the internal temperature must be at 165 degrees to be food safe. Have fun!

A BRIEF DIATRIBE ON THANKSGIVING DINNER

(ACCORDING TO JIM)

Inspired Magazine October November 2010

Let's talk turkey.

Contrary to popular belief, Thanksgiving was not invented by the National Football League to sell another days worth of beer advertising. It is, however, a traditional American holiday during which families and friends from all over the United States gather together once a year to catch up and eat dinner at the same time: halftime…ha! (And sometimes once a year is far too often!)

Traditionally as well, the star attraction of the feast is none other than our Native American fowl, the turkey. My lovely wife, Brenda, and I have hosted Thanksgiving dinner for probably the last 25 years. It is not unusual to have 50 or 60 people show up including both sides of the family, friends, as well as a couple reprobates of society thrown into the fray. That amount of humanity necessitates a large quantity of food and drink. A couple of fresh, not frozen, 20-pound-plus turkeys and a ham the size of a small car engine are always on the roster.

How DO you do it, you ask? Well, since we have been doing this extravaganza so long, I keep trying to come up with new ways to prepare the upcoming meal. First: get help. Especially when you're combining turkey and hot oil, like we did two years ago.

On Wednesday, Thanksgiving Eve, our daughter Fawn came over to help prep. While Brenda tidied up the house, Fawn and I toasted up six loaves of white and whole wheat bread. Chop! Chop! Chop! Our knives flew through the bread, fresh mushrooms, celery, red onions, and cloves of the stinky rose, garlic. It was human vegematic at its best.

I set about prepping our big birds. Turkey number one I submersed in a kosher saltwater brine with sliced up oranges, lemons, and limes. Turkey number two was destined to be the star attraction. We were going to deep fat fry it the next day on the east deck. So I made up a concoction of apple juice, onion juice, garlic juice, and Cajun seasoning and with a syringe, injected it all throughout the bird. We then rubbed the entire bird with Cajun seasoning and put it to rest for the night.

Early Thanksgiving morning, I put coffee on and started working on our brined turkey. After patting it dry, I laid it on its back and gently worked my hands under the skin covering the breasts. Once the skin was loosened up, I placed pads of butter and fresh sage leaves underneath. We were good to go. Into the oven at 425 degrees for 20 minutes, breast side down. I turned it over on its back and reduced the heat to 325 degrees. Rule of thumb with a bird this size is to cook it for fifteen minutes a pound. I always check, however. You want to insert a meat thermometer into the thigh meat and have it read 165 degrees and have the juices run clear. Try not to overcook it or you will have a dried disaster on your hands. Trust me, I have been there.

Time to finish the stuffing.

Three pounds of fried, drained pork sausage, a dozen whipped eggs, enough chicken stock to make it moist, a little dried sage, and some salt and fresh ground black pepper all went into the mixture. Into a roaster covered with aluminum foil at about 200 degrees. Whew! Time for a cup of coffee with cream. The adrenaline was starting to kick in. A lot of prep lay ahead and time was growing shorter.

The ham was next on the agenda: cut a crisscross pattern, place it in a roaster, cover with pineapple slices and baste with rosé wine.

Back to baste turkey number one, then on to the spectacle: my outside cooker. You probably have seen those outside turkey cookers advertised on TV complete with a perforated stainless steel basket to lower the turkey into the hot oil. Well, our setup is a little more sophisticated. My outside cooker is about waist high. Add to that a tall pot. Add peanut oil about halfway up. The trick is enough oil to cover turkey number two but not enough to boil over. We straighten out a wire coat hanger and truss up the turkey's legs with one end. We then make a loop on the other end. When the oil is at 360 degrees on a candy thermometer, it is time to give our fowl a soothing oil bubble bath. At high noon, the two sons of the family, Shanon and Conor, climb up the ladders with a broom handle inserted through the wire loop and gently lower the turkey into the churning froth. Talk about shanty Irish!

Back inside to baste.

Fawn, thank God, showed up just in time to help peel and cook 40 pounds of potatoes and help concoct a salad of iceberg and spring mix lettuces, red onions, green peppers, green and black olives, tomatoes, grapes, strawberries, and feta cheese. Guests started to arrive bearing side dishes, desserts and beverages of their choice.

Pretty soon every counter in the kitchen was covered with delectable delights.

I started the potatoes boiling then went to check on our boiling bird. Not quite ready. It takes about three minutes a pound to cook. When the turkey floats, it is good to go, but always do that check with a meat thermometer. Back in the house, I made gravy and quickly mashed the potatoes. The time had grown near to pull this all together.

Brenda had decorated marvelously, and also had brought out every plate in the house along with all of the silverware and wineglasses. We

pulled the turkeys and ham and placed them on platters. While they rested for ten minutes, we gathered everyone together and my brother, Pat, led us in a prayer of thanks. Three of us started carving, plates began filling, and pretty soon every available seat in the house was occupied. Even the steps leading upstairs were filled with some of the younger folk. It was a feeding frenzy. Seconds, Thirds. An hour later, it was all over but the crying. Except for cleanup, of course….

Brenda, her sisters, and sister in-law stepped up to the plate, er plates, and in no time reduced a mountain of dishes into oblivion. The rest of us sipped our beverages contentedly, engaged in small talk, played cards, slept, and occasionally watched on TV guys with helmets and shoulder pads beat up on each other. With a glass of wine in hand, I mused to my brother in-law "You know if Benjamin Franklin had had his way, the national bird of the country would have been the turkey. That means a certain football team from Pennsylvania might have called the Philadelphia Turkeys. Now there is food for thought." Speaking of food, it was time to start a second round and dive into the leftovers. Nothing like a cold turkey or ham sandwich. Ah, life is good.

GERDA (MOM) AND JIM'S HOMEMADE STUFFING

1-1 lb. loaf white cottage bread	6 celery stalks, chopped fine
1 lb. Ground pork sausage	Salt/Fresh ground black pepper
1-1 lb. loaf whole wheat bread	1 large onion, diced
4 oz. slivered almonds 8 oz. fresh mushrooms, sliced	3 large eggs, whisked
Ground dried sage	4 garlic cloves, minced 32 oz. chicken broth

Toast bread and cut into ½ inch pieces. In a large mixing bowl, combine toast, mushrooms, celery, onions, and garlic. Fry up sausage and drain. Add to mixture along with almonds. Lightly season with sage, salt, and pepper. Toss and season again. Repeat twice more. Add eggs and mix thoroughly. Add chicken broth and mix well. Bake in oven in a large covered casserole dish at 325 degrees for 1 ½ to 2 hours. Stuffing is ready when the middle reaches 165 degrees. (Serves 12-16)

WE'RE HAVING A PARTY
(LOCATION: SOUTHERN PROVENCE)

Inspired Magazine December 2010/January 2011

In my opinion, the important things in life are the experiences, not material goods. The memories of those experiences you carry with you for life. And wonderful memories were certainly made when my wife, Brenda, and I traveled with friends to the south of France last September. We had rented a mountainside villa for two weeks, complete with an infinity pool, surrounded by vineyards, and overlooking the Mediterranean Sea. I know! I know! Life, sometimes, can be extremely cruel. Our traveling companions were our dear friends, Jack and Sheryl, from Connecticut, and Sheryl's cousin, Lisa, from Florida. Jack and Sheryl picked us up at the Marseille airport and we headed to Le Beausset, the closest town to our villa. It was to be Jack and Sheryl's 25th wedding anniversary the next day. A party had been planned and it was time to procure provisions. Let's see. 25 or so bottles of wine to be added to the couple of cases Jack had already purchased at the neighborhood wine co-op. Two kinds of paté, olives, three types of crackers, fish balls, nuts, an assortment of cold thin slices of French hard sausages, duck breast (canard), garlic cloves, potatoes, salad mixings, six different cheeses, and, of course, loaves and loaves of French baguettes.

We packed ourselves and purchases into our rental car and headed up the mountain. A hair-raising experience to say the least. The road was barely wide enough for two vehicles to pass one another. With lots of blind corners and cars whipping by at 100 kilometers an hour, I started to contemplate the sanity of our journey here. Once we reached our villa, however, and the trembling had subsided. The view itself made it all worthwhile.

Time for some wine to savor in the magnificence of the surrounding countryside. We were in the Bandol area of Southern France which is famous for its rosé vintages. We uncorked a bottle and clinked glasses to toast the fading sunset. Lisa arrived after spending the day with her and Sheryl's cousins who live in Le Plan, about 10 kilometers away over the mountain. By this time we were all hungry, so Sheryl put together a wonderful tomato-based vegetarian spaghetti. In the process, she also "painted" the kitchen wall and ceiling red. A little wine consumption may have been the culprit here.

A gorgeous, sunlit morning arrived on anniversary day. Much to our surprise, Didier and Shirley, owners of the villa, had hung a large welcome sign to all of us on the carport. I love this country! We lounged leisurely by the pool reading and taking in the rays. After

all, one had to be fully rested and energized to prepare to take part in the traditional French five-course meal planned for the anniversary extravaganza. Things started heating up at about two in the afternoon. The sound of feet tramping up the driveway caught our attention. Bernard, who is married to Annette, (Sheryl and Lisa's cousin) and Didier were lugging up a 12-foot table that was to hold the appetizers and drinks. It was time to get on with the business

of the day. Brenda and Lisa decorated and set tables under the carport. Sheryl concocted a fabulous salad complete with an olive oil and balsamic vinegar dressing. The main featured attraction was to be grilled duck breast. Each breast weighed about ten ounces. Now those were some big ducks. Bernard, a tremendous cook, had the responsibility of preparing and finishing that dish. He made a simple but wonderful marinade (recipe to follow). He then made six horizontal slits on the bottom side of each breast and inserted flat slices of garlic into them. I love this country! The breasts were set aside for a couple of hours, happily swimming in and soaking up marinade. Didier, in the meantime, had slipped away to his studio across the driveway and came back with a small keg of Heineken beer. This was a pleasant surprise, very refreshing and a perfect accompaniment to the chores of the afternoon. My contribution to the festive occasion was to be a potato dish. A sort of simple version of a potato galette. We had picked up some waxy yellow skinned white potatoes. I sliced them into quarter-inch rounds and laid them in single rows overlapping each other in an olive oil-coated rectangular metal baking dish. I then sprinkled some freshly minced garlic on top and drizzled on a mixture of melted butter and olive oil. A dusting of fleur de sel (sea salt) and freshly ground black pepper and we were good to go. Well, almost. It seems that this Irish American who can barely mumble 10 words in French, much less read anything, was about to be put to the test. The oven in the kitchen was an electric convection oven. (Never used one of appliances before, much less with instructions in French). Woe is me! I scratched my brain for about a half of an hour until I had to admit defeat and find Didier to come to the rescue. To further complicate the issue, the heat settings were measured in Celsius, of course, not Fahrenheit. Despite Didier's comprehensive knowledge of the English language it still took us three tries over the next half of an hour to achieve the proper baking temperature. Well, at least there was some great male bonding.

While the great oven debacle was going on, guests began arriving and it was time to begin what turned out to be a wonderful three-hour meal. Appetizers covered the table along with wine and cocktails. There were 18 of us in all, cousins and friends of Jack and Sheryl, all there to celebrate their 25 years together. We all mingled and tried to understand each other despite our language differences. When it came time to sit down, Sheryl had decided to have salad as the second course before the main meal. In France, it is tradition to have salad after the main course. That Sheryl, she always has been the renegade. Bernard's canard grilled to perfection at medium rare followed, accompanied by Jimmy Mac's finally baked potatoes, and wine, of course. There are over 400 different types of cheeses produced in France and we sampled six with white wine for the next course. After the cheese tray had made it around the table four or five times, it was time for dessert. Annette had made a wonderful creamy meringue cake that, of course, was accompanied by what else? More wine.

After three hours of wining and dining it was now time for the party to really begin. The music was cranked up. People started dancing. Bernard and Didier began boisterous rounds of singing French ballads. More wine, more wine. Dance, dance. Sing, sing.

Laugh until you can't take it any more. The wee hours of the morning approach and guests slowly begin to fade away into the countryside. But not first without tremendous hugs and kissing of both cheeks. It is tradition, of course. Finally only the five of us remain. A final toast to Jack and Sheryl. Cheers. God, I love this country!

BERNARD'S CANARD

Marinade Duck
1 cup honey
4 8-10 oz skinless duck breasts
6 oz fish sauce

8-10 garlic cloves
6 oz soy sauce
¼ cup extra virgin olive oil

Combine marinade ingredients and whisk. Set aside.
Remove garlic husks. Slice cloves vertically into very thin flat pieces. Cut six slots on the bottom of each breast. Insert garlic pieces in each slot. Marinate breasts for at least one hour.

Grill over medium heat 3-4 minutes a side until medium rare. (Reddish pink inside).

INSPIRED MAGAZINE 2011

MOM, MOTHER'S DAY, AND RHUBARB
(OR THE UPSIDE UPSIDE DOWN CAKE)

Inspired Magazine Spring 2011

S oon winter will be just a *sleeting* memory. With the advent of spring comes an ever-changing cornucopia of newly-sprouting varieties of vegetation. Lilies of the Valley, Fiddlehead Ferns, Dutchman's Breeches, Bluebells, and Jack in the Pulpit abound in the woods around the Driftless Region. One finds the spark of new life in the cultivated gardens of the area as well. Asparagus loves to nudge its pointy little head out of the earth at the first advent of frost packing it in for another season. Freshly planted onion sets strive mightily to reach out and touch the sun. Lettuces frolic with wild abandon, seemingly screaming out "Pick me! Pick me! And slather me with homemade Green Goddess dressing!" But the most formidable spring garden plant just has to be rhubarb. Once it takes hold, it is just like the Energizer bunny. It keeps growing and growing and growing.

So let me share a story from the McCaffrey Family Chronicles. A tale of rhubarb deception or at the very least, a mother's indiscretion. I grew up the son of a father who went through the Great Depression and a mother who escaped with her sister from East Germany during World War Two. Together my parents some how came up with the down payment on an 80-acre farm just west of Decorah. I'm sure making the ends meet while raising five children and sending them to the Catholic school as well was no picnic in the park. After all, my dad was a rural mail carrier and like most families at that time, he was the sole wage earner. In order to make do, we had a couple of large gardens and raised various species of livestock that graced the table throughout the year. One year we raised 400 chickens in the garage. We spent an entire weekend butchering and pulling feathers. We then proceeded to have chicken for supper six days a week. On the seventh day we rested and had hamburger. I still do like chicken in spite of that experience. Needless to say, a lot of effort was necessary to keep the farm above the waterline.

We pretty much lived out of the gardens year-round. What wasn't eaten fresh was preserved in one fashion or another. Potatoes and onions were piled on pallets in a dark abyss of a corner in the basement. To this day I can remember distinctly the raw spud aroma that permeated the basement air. Hey, my father was Irish, so 400 pounds of potatoes hanging out in the basement was not uncommon. We also amassed a trove of canned vegetables and pickles that were stored in a large floor-to-ceiling cupboard in the cellar.

Mom was the "preserve principal" in our family. She had a small wooden-handled paring knife that she used for her culinary cutups. As a chef I marvel at the amount of food she processed with that knife. Bushels of sweet corn were voided of their kernels by several swift strokes. She spent hours at the kitchen table being the human vegematic. I can just see her slicing strawberries, chopping up rhubarb, and cutting green beans French style.

Rhubarb was usually the first of the yearly harvest. Mom would slice the stalks into small pieces and freeze most of them for when the strawberries were ripe and delicious. She then made some delicious strawberry and rhubarb jam and pies. My favorite of her desserts, however, was her so-called Rhubarb Upside Down Cake with a sweet butter sauce. Mom passed away a couple years ago and no one can find that recipe. I decided to use some Irish ingenuity and see if I could come up with something close. So I Googled Best Rhubarb Upside Down Cake. "What is wrong with this picture?" In fact, "PICTURES." Every recipe with a picture of the cake had the rhubarb on top. Even Martha Stewart's. (One can't argue with America's culinary maven). Mom's rhubarb was on the bottom. My childhood conception of upside down cake has been completely shattered. Mom, how could you have led me so astray? OK. Take a deep breath and breathe easy, breathe easy. Time to come up with a plan. In the future, I will call it Rhubarb Upside Upside down cake and the heck with Martha. I plan on making this for my family in honor of my mom on Mother's Day this year. It isn't the original recipe but it is close. Oh, and Mom, I still love you.

RHUBARB UPSIDE UPSIDE DOWN CAKE

8 Tbl butter	4 cups all purpose flour
1 1/2 cups packed brown sugar	2 Tbl baking powder
8 cups cut up rhubarb	2 cups milk
3/4 cup butter	3 eggs
2 cups granulated sugar	1 Tbl vanilla

Preheat oven to 350 degrees. Melt 8 Tbl butter in large skillet or pot.

Add brown sugar and stir until blended. Add rhubarb and mix until well coated.

Grease an 11 X 18 baking dish. Cover the bottom evenly with rhubarb mixture.

Cream butter with sugar in an electric mixer. Add the rest of the ingredients.

Mix until smooth. Gently pour over the rhubarb mixture and smooth with a rubber spatula. Bake 40-50 minutes until toothpick inserted in the center comes out clean.

SWEET BUTTER SAUCE

1 cup butter	1 cup cream or 1/2 and 1/2
2 cups sugar	2 tsp vanilla

Combine all ingredients in a sauce pan on medium low.

Cook and stir for about 10 minutes or until sugar is dissolved.

Pour warm over cake slices and enjoy!

WHAT THE #@&--- IS MIREPOIX?

Inspired Magazine Summer 2011

If I had to name my favorite comfort food I would have to proclaim a category, not a single dish. Or plate or bowl for that matter. I am simply unable to narrow it down. Impossible! But I do really like soup. No, no. Let's change that: I love soup! Hot soup, cold soup, cream based soup, no holds barred soup, etc. You get the picture. At the restaurant I wear a multitude of different hats. One of them happens to be the chief soupmiester. In other words, I makea dah soup. Actually, three to four soups a week. We have a "two soups at all times" goal. Heartier soups in the cold months and lighter soups as the seasons bloom into warmth, but one soup remains constant: Every Friday I make a new batch of seafood chowder. The rest of the time it is up for grabs. A balancing act ensues as we try new recipes and also try to fulfill requests for previously prepared potages. And sometimes, if we are really busy and the soup's sailing out the kitchen, it becomes an Irish scramble just to put something presentable and delicious in the bowls.

All that being said, let's look at what it takes to make good, (ah great), soup: A balance of the freshest ingredients available – preferably local – and flavor, flavor, flavor. Or, in other words – onion, celery, carrots. Leave it to the French to concoct the perfect base to enhance stocks, sauces, soups, stews, roasts, and a myriad of other dishes. Mirepoix is the common name for this base. Sometimes referred to as the "Holy Trinity" of French cuisine, it's a mixture of aromatics: two parts chopped onion to one part each of chopped carrot and celery. It can be utilized either raw, roasted, or sautéed. When making stocks, mirepoix is normally roasted to add more flavor and color – that works well for brown stocks. Parsnips can, and often are, substituted for the carrots for clear stocks. Since the mirepoix is removed at the end of stock making, one can make the case for the old saying "Size does not matter". Well, for chopped vegetables anyway. Uniform pieces are ideal, so everything is cooked evenly. Smaller pieces cook in less time and tend to emit more flavor.

For most cream based soups the mirepoix is run through a food processor and blended into the featured ingredient. (ie: Cream of Broccoli, Cream of Tomato, etc.). So that allows for bigger chunks and less chopping. For soup, traditionally the mirepoix is sautéed in butter. Ah, those French again! I, myself, prefer to use extra virgin olive oil. Either way is perfectly acceptable for a great end product. Olive oil just makes it easier for the lactose intolerant and imparts a wonderful flavor of its own.

Also, not being a traditionalist and more of a renegade, I always add fresh minced garlic.

Garlic is good, garlic is great, garlic makes the world go round. That is one of the great presents my dad gave to me. I still have fond memories of working in the family garden and Dad pulling up a bulb of garlic, breaking off a couple of cloves, and sharing one with me while expounding upon the great health benefits of eating raw garlic every day. A little warm Old Style helped to offset the stinky rose's pungency. Hey, everybody's family is a little dysfunctional.

Ok, time to don our Julia Child frocks and go to work. First pour a glass of your favorite wine or beverage. Savor a sip or two. Relax. Breathe slowly. Proceed with the following recipe and continue savoring throughout.

Since we are heading into the summer gardening season, I decided a fresh cream of tomato and basil soup would be just the ticket to round out this sojourn into basic cooking techniques. Fresh plum tomatoes work well here as they are meatier than most and make for a thicker soup. You can parboil them for 20 to 30 seconds to remove the skins if so desired for a more creamy variation. If you want to make this soup when fresh from the garden tomatoes are not available, substitute one 28-ounce can of whole plum or crushed tomatoes for every two pounds of tomatoes. So let's savor a little more wine then take our creation to another level by adding some bleu cheese right at the end. Some crunchy French bread, candlelight, probably a little more wine, and your significant other will be marveling at your culinary genius. Congratulations, you have now mastered French Cooking 101, or at least the Mirepoix section. Julia would have been proud. Next time perhaps we will work on foie gras.

But, for now, as Julia always said, "Bon Appetit!"

CREAM OF TOMATO BASIL SOUP WITH BLEU CHEESE

(Serves 4)

2 tablespoons extra virgin oil

1 rib celery, washed and diced

1 small carrot, peeled and diced

1 medium onion, diced

2 garlic cloves, minced

2 pounds fresh tomatoes,
   peeled, seeded and chopped

1 tablespoon tomato paste

2 cups chicken broth or water

2 tablespoons fresh minced basil

1cup heavy cream

1-2 ounces fresh crumbled bleu
   cheese

Kosher salt and fresh ground black
   pepper to taste

In a large stainless steel or nonstick saucepan, add olive oil over medium heat. Add celery and carrot. Sautee for three to four minutes until softened. Add onion and garlic. Sautee two to three minutes until onion starts to turn translucent. Add tomatoes, tomato paste, broth and basil. Bring to a boil and reduce heat to low. Cover, stir frequently at a simmer for fifteen minutes. Puree soup in a food processor or blender in batches. Reheat in saucepan. Stir in heavy cream Add bleu cheese and season to taste with salt and pepper. Simmer once more until soup is hot to taste. Serve with crusty French bread. Enjoy!

TIS' THE SEASON...TAILGAITING SEASON, THAT IS

Inspired Magazine Fall 2011

Now that summer is an outgoing tide of memories, it is time to ratchet it up for the next big thing. It's party central. Step up and rub shoulders with the big boys and/or... er, girls... as well. Football mania is descending upon us and with it comes another national pastime: tailgating. This social phenomenon is kind of like the Energizer Bunny. Starting in August with preseason NFL games and concluding in early February with the Super Bowl, the season keeps going and going and going. And with it comes pre-game get-togethers with family,

friends, and inevitably, total strangers. I would imagine the ritual probably dates back to at least the ancient Greek Olympic Games with buddies sharing six packs of mead and lamb kabobs. The best rendition of its beginning I could find, after a little digging, was in 1919. It was Green Bay's first year and fans backed their pickups around the field and used their tailgates as seats to watch the games. As a Packer fan, that scenario made the appeal of tailgating infinitely clearer.

So let's get started. The first and most important

item to procure is a boatload of your favorite adult beverage. Ice-cold beer works well here. I would suggest not bringing a case of Dom Pérignon champagne – everybody will think you're a snob. Remember – these events began in the back of a truck… but still try to put your own spin on it. Local foods and local beers are welcome, and when outdoors, cans are usually best… and make sure you bring enough to share! (Fun aside, it is also important to drink responsibly – you still have to get home from the party. When in doubt, call a cab!)

To work up an appetite, toss the beat up old football around and enjoy a couple turns playing hacky sack or the beanbag game with the kids. One needs to prepare for the smorgasbord of food that is being spread out on the beer pong table. What was once probably just a simple pre-game lunch of hotdogs and hamburgers has evolved into a treasure trove of tasty treats. I love it – especially the common sharing of food by everyone. Old family recipes like someone's mom's dill pickles proudly and inevitably show up on the table. Homemade fresh salsa and chips, potato salad, coleslaw, a seven layer Mexican casserole dip, baked beans and, of course, deviled eggs, are frequent sides awaiting a cornucopia of grilled goodies from the barbeque virtuosos.

It is not uncommon for these masters of the heat to be set up at dawn and slow cooking or smoking their delicious fare. Each one an MVP in their own right. Kings of the coals. Bragging rights are at stake here. There is something about playing with fire that brings out the primal beast in all of us. But that's part of the fun of it all. The grill guys are putting on a show, pumping out ribs, hot and spicy barbeque chicken wings, root

beer pulled pork, bratwurst, shrimp kabobs, and the list goes on and on. The camaraderie is infectious. Fans from opposing sides sitting together gently ribbing each other about their teams, discussing the finer points of previous games, and having a gastronomic marathon.

Tailgating parties aren't necessarily limited to the parking lots of your team's stadiums either. Can't make it to the game? Pull a television out into the garage or deck. Invite family and friends to bring their respective grills and side dishes. This actually has some advantages. Since this is a private party, you can control who shows up. You do not have to put up with the obnoxious guy who has to prove how macho he is by going around smashing beer cans on his forehead. Unless, of course, he is your brother-in-law. Then you are just out of luck. All kidding aside, tailgating at home can be a very enjoyable experience. A simple thing I like to do is grill sweet corn. Since I am not on a first name basis with Martha Stewart I will have to give her credit for this idea. Husk your sweet corn and put it on the grill on high heat. Keep turning until the corn is nicely browned on all sides. Melt some butter and add fresh lime juice and cayenne pepper to it. Slather on corn and enjoy.

Have fun with the whipping up the following sides, and try my famous grilled chicken recipe (you might remember this from my Father's Day 2010 column)! The food options are virtually endless…

Uh oh! Gotta run. It's game time!

CAROLINA COLESLAW

(Serves 8-10)

Dressing:

1 tsp dry mustard

1 tsp celery seed
1 cup apple cider vinegar

1 cup sugar

1 tsp salt

2/3 cup canola oil

Combine following ingredients in a large bowl:

1 head of cabbage, finely shredded

1 Vidalia onion, finely chopped

2 carrots, grated

In a sauce pan, add all dressing ingredients. Bring to a boil over medium heat. Simmer and stir over medium heat until sugar is dissolved. Cool and pour over veggies and toss. Refrigerate until cold.

GERDA'S POTATO SALAD (THANKS MOM!)

5 lbs. Russet or Idaho potatoes

4 garlic cloves, minced

1 dozen hard boiled eggs

1 1/2 cups mayonnaise

1 small red onion, diced fine

1/4 cup yellow mustard

4 stalks celery, diced fine

2 Tbl Dijon mustard

2-3 large dill pickles, diced fine

2 Tbl spicy brown mustard

6 radishes sliced thin Salt and pepper to taste

Peel and dice potatoes. Boil until just tender. Drain and cool. Separate egg yolks from whites. Place yolks in a medium sized bowl. Mash into small pieces. Stir in garlic, mayonnaise, and mustards. Chop egg whites into small pieces and place in a large mixing bowl. Stir in remaining vegetables. Gently stir in mayonnaise mixture until well combined. Season to taste with salt and pepper. Refrigerate until cold 4-6 hours.

GRILLED ROADSIDE CHICKEN

(Serves four)

1 3 lb chicken (cut into 8 pcs)

2 bunches green onions

1 ½ tsp ancho chile powder

1 teaspoon Mexican oregano

¼ tsp ground cloves

¼ tsp cinnamon

2 cloves garlic, minced

3 T apple cider vinegar

¼ cup orange juice

1 tsp salt

Wash chicken with cold water and pat dry with paper towels. Place in a 9x13 baking dish. Trim green onions of any wilted leaves and roots. Set aside. Combine remaining ingredients to make a marinade. Coat all sides of the chicken with marinade. Let rest for 30 minutes. The chicken should be grilled over indirect heat. If using a gas grill, light the outside burners and leave the center one off. With a charcoal grill, push the grill ready coals to one side. You will have to add more coals about half way through.

Place chicken on the non-heated portion of the grill. Cook without turning. Baste occasionally with remaining marinade. Chicken is ready when juices run clear. (About 45 minutes). About 10 minutes before chicken is ready brush green onions with vegetable or olive and place over direct heat until tender. Place chicken on cutting board and cover with foil for 10 minutes. Serve two pieces per person with grilled onions on top.

HOLY HOT DISH!!!

Inspired Magazine Winter 2011

Sometimes the stars seem to align at just the right time. So it was this fall when Aryn and I talked topics for the winter Mississippi Mirth. It was unanimous: With the holidays fast approaching and leftovers awaiting, the ultimate comfort food – the casserole – would be perfect! And, as a matter of fact, I happen to have a bit of knowledge on casseroles. In my cookbook, "Midwest Cornfusion," (published in 2006) I

devoted an entire chapter these delectable baked dishes, and the following is the introduction:

"The State Dish of Minnesota

Never let it be said that the good citizens of Minnesota are a few peas short of a full casserole. They just think it adds too much color to the tuna dish. All over Minnesota, at hundreds of church gatherings, potlucks are as entrenched in the tradition and culture as blond hair and Paul Bunyan and "Babe" the Blue Ox. The casserole divas come out in droves to fill up church basements with their favorite concoctions. These are shared communally with other members of their congregations. In Minnesota (actually the only Scandinavian country located within the continental United States) these creations are widely known as "Hot Dish".

And up to a couple years ago, these hot dish happenings were "above the law". It seems that holding these public gatherings with food brought in from non-state inspected kitchens was in violation of food safety ordinances. Mostly, the food police turned a blind eye to these "illegal" activities. However, not always. Al Juhnke, who happened to be a state senator, was turned away at the door of a Democrat/Farmer/Labor (DFL) gathering and told to take his crockpot back to his car. Annoyed, he got a "Hot Dish" bill passed to exempt organization potlucks from state food handling regulations. The Sons of Norway rejoiced. No longer were they outlaws in the North Star State.

So have a little fun. Go crazy. Add some green peas to that tuna casserole and maybe even a red pepper or two. You may be the hurrah of the hot dish hullabaloo."

You may be relieved to know that last session the Minnesota legislature passed "The Church Lady Bill" which exempted faith based groups from routine state health inspections at events where food is being served to large masses of people. (However, it stipulated that at least one person involved in these large food functions must have completed a state-approved training seminar in large crowd food preparation.)

Not coincidentally, large crowds are a casserole specialty: one can feed a lot of people for very little expense. Casseroles were extremely popular during the Great Depression for that very reason. It also helped that Campbell's rolled out condensed mushroom soup in 1934.

Although casseroles are commonly known in Minnesota as the "Lutheran Binder" because it is found en mass in church cookbooks, Lutherans aren't the only group with bragging rights. The Catholics are in on it as well. My mother, God bless her soul, was an extremely devout Catholic. Which meant that on Fridays we didn't eat meat. Which also meant that for 20 years on almost every Friday we had tuna casserole. Noodles, tuna, and mushroom soup with some saltine crackers broken up on top just to pizzazz it up a little. Man, we were living in hot dish heaven. (No offense Mom, just a little Irish humor.)

But, I digress. Let's really get to the meat of this casserole phenomenon.

I did a little more research. Casserole comes from the French word, casse, meaning small saucepan. The main difference between casseroles and stews is that stews are cooked with heat coming from the bottom of the dish while casseroles are surrounded by heat in the oven. And I know you will all be devastated (like me) to know your favorite green bean casserole recipe that your mother passed down to you was not your mother's recipe at all. Truth be told, it came off of the back of a Durkee French Fried Onion container. Geesh, Mom!

In my own family, it has been said that a good marriage is like a casserole. Only those involved know what goes into it. My lovely wife, Brenda, and I have been married for almost 32 years. And over that timespan we have made a lot of casseroles. On the weekends it was not unusual to have 10 or 15 kids over visiting our three children. One of Brenda's favorite casseroles to make was a goulash (recipe to follow). Except it wasn't the traditional goulash of the Czech

Republic. Instead of having big chunks of beef or pork in it, she used ground beef. I asked her if she got the recipe passed down from her Czech mother. She said she couldn't remember. I suspect it was off the back of a Durkee French Fried Onion container. My favorite casserole to make then, and still now, is Chicken Cacciatore (recipe to follow). In the early 80s, when we owned The Café Deluxe, we would sometimes make it for our lunch special. We often had 40 servings sell out in just half an hour.

Chicken Cacciatore is an Italian dish made "hunter-style". The story behind it is a hunter came home from the woods empty handed except for a few measly mushrooms. His wife created this dish for him. Lucky guy. And lucky all of us as well.

So you see casseroles usually aren't complicated, but they are fun to make (you can even have your kids help!) and are on the table quicker than you can say "What's for dinner?" Ah, yes, Comfort Food. Living the dream! And don't be afraid to experiment a little. Who says your Hot Dish can't be a "Haute Dish"?

BRENDA'S GOULASH

8 oz. macaroni noodles

1 lb. 85 percent ground beef

29 oz. can diced tomatoes

14 1/2 oz. can tomato soup

1 large onion, diced

1 large green pepper, diced

2-3 cloves garlic, minced

Salt and fresh ground black to taste

¼ cup olive oil

Preheat oven to 350 degrees. Cook noodles according to directions on the package. Drain. Brown ground beef in a large pot. Drain and add back to the pot. Add noodles and the rest of the ingredients. Stir well. Brush an 11"x19" Pyrex baking dish with the olive oil. Empty the pot into the baking dish. Bake uncovered for about 20 minutes or until tomatoes are bubbly.

CHICKEN CACCIATORE

8 oz spaghetti

1/4 cup water

1/4 cup flour

1/4 cup sliced ripe olives

1 tsp salt

1 medium onion, chopped

1/4 teaspoon black pepper

2 cloves garlic, minced

4 lb chicken cut into 8 pieces

1 tsp salt

1/4 cup olive oil

1 tsp crushed dried oregano

16 oz can tomatoes

1/4 tsp pepper

8 oz can tomato sauce

1 bay leaf

1 cup sliced mushrooms

Snipped parsley

1/4 cup olive oil

Preheat oven to 350 degrees. Boil spaghetti according to package directions. Mix flour,1 tsp salt, and ¼ teaspoon black pepper. Dredge chicken pieces in flour mixture. In a 12-inch skillet heat oil until hot. Fry chicken on all sides until brown, about 15 minutes. Remove to a plate and reserve. Put all remaining ingredients back in skillet except parsley, heat to boiling and breakup tomatoes with a fork. Grease an 11x18 Pyrex baking dish with remaining olive oil. Fill bottom with spaghetti noodles. Nest chicken pieces on spaghetti. Ladle tomato mixture over each piece.

Cover with aluminum foil and bake until thickest pieces are cooked thoroughly, about thirty minutes (165 degrees on a thermometer). Plate up and garnish with parsley.

(Note: This recipe is an adaptation of a recipe found in Betty Crocker's International Cookbook pg 87, copyright 1980).

INSPIRED MAGAZINE 2012

TAPAS TALK
Inspired Magazine Spring 2012

I n 1976 my childhood and lifelong friend, James Ronan, and I decided that in order to celebrate the 200th anniversary of the founding of the United States of America, we would travel to Southern Europe. We would immerse ourselves in some of the diverse cultures that have combined to make up our vast country. In other words, we were looking to party hearty. As opposed to working for a living, seven weeks of backpacking, traveling by train, and hanging out in youth hostels seemed like nirvana. So we both went out and bought ourselves a bible.

Not the King James version. Arthur Frommer's version. Europe on Five Dollars a Day. No self-respecting backpacker would be without a copy.

However, it was almost the trip that wasn't. We were going to fly on Icelandic Airlines out of O'Hare. We caught a ride with our good friends, Bruce and Karen, and stayed overnight in the suburbs. In the morning we got up and got moving. All of a sudden I heard a "What the H…?!?" from James. It turns out that his passport and wallet were missing. They were conveniently sitting on Bruce's coffee table back in Decorah. It would be impossible to make a mad dash back to Decorah and return in time for the 5 pm boarding. James called Bruce's then-roommate Steve Matter (Quality Chicks) and somehow convinced him to go on a road trip. Dave Stanley rode shotgun. They made it with 10 minutes to spare. Whew, that was close! After profusely thanking our knights in shining armor, we boarded and headed toward Luxemburg.

We didn't have a clue of what we should be doing. We met a young woman on the plane headed to Paris. So we tagged along. In Paris we procured some cheese, baguettes, and wine at a little neighborhood grocery and headed to a youth hostel. There we ran into a young man from Australia named Sandy Aich. He had, unbelievable as this may seem, an ITINERY. In the morning we hooked up with him at breakfast and decided that an organized plan was much better than no plan at all. Sandy was headed to Boudreaux and on to the southern half of Europe. We left Paris without even checking out a museum, a church, or Pere Lachaise Cemetery (final resting place of the late great Jim Morrison). Like I said, we didn't have a clue.

After a great day in Boudreaux sightseeing and drinking delicious wine we headed to Zaragoza, Spain where our friends, Jim and Janice, were living. Getting there was, to say the least, a little bit hairy and scary. At the French and Spanish border we had to change trains. The train track

in Spain was of a different width then that of the French. It was midnight and the train station is deserted, locked, and out in the middle of nowhere. The three of us sat on benches outside the station, smoked cigarettes, and try to be nonchalant. Definitely not on Sandy's ITINERY. Finally a passenger train backed into the station. We boarded. It had old wooden seats out of the 1900s. No heat but at least we were moving. Well, sort of. Two hours later at 3 am, the train stopped in the middle of another nowhere, surrounded by the La Guardia, the national military police. They were holding sub machine guns and ordering everyone off the train along with baggage. Our backpacks were ripped open and contents dumped unceremoniously onto the desert dirt. All we could do was just sit there and hold our breath. Finally, we moved out again to Madrid, where Jim and Janice picked us up. It was certainly good to see familiar faces.

Zaragoza was to be home for me for the next 10 days. We made our way there, where Janice had made us some supper and then it was time to check out the local bar scene. They lived in an upstairs apartment and around the corner was a small bar called the Cosa del Sol, open 24/7. Owned by three brothers, each worked an eight-hour shift everyday. Talk about dedication. Upon walking in I was struck by all the food laid out on the bar and smoked hams dried in nets hanging from the ceiling. There were seven or eight types of huge olives along with several different types of cheese, sardines, anchovies, crusty breads, small chorizo sausages, and shrimp. I thought I had died and gone to heaven. I wanted to try everything right then and

there. So I pretty much did. This was one of the many tapas – or finger food – bars found all over Spain. You make up a small plate, order a drink and repeat, repeat, repeat. Sometimes the food is free, sometimes there is a small charge. The tapas differ from town to town and area to area. One of the best at the Cosa del Sol was fabulous homemade onion rings they kept churning out hour after hour. I've never had better.

James and Sandy decided to go to Toledo and then on to Morocco for a few days. I wanted to take in the locals and hang out with Jim and Janice. So while Jim was working I spent time at the Cosa del Sol. I got to know the regulars. We shared a lot of laughs.

Most of them were retired and the Cosa del Sol was their social club. Turned out to be mine as well. They were all interested in the political scene in the US. I also got to know the bar owner brothers and their families. I had long hair down to the small of my back and a pretty good beard. One of the brother's sons came up to me, touched my hair and said "Boofalo Bill". That became my handle for the rest of my stay. On my last day, the regulars decided they wanted to show me the town. This involved taking me around to all of the tapas bars in probably a 12-block area for a small glass of wine and a small bite. There were a lot of tapas bars in that area. My favorite served one of the national dishes of Spain called the Spanish Tortilla. (Recipe to follow). It is simple and wonderful.

Clueless as James and I were, we had a wonderful experience and it is time to thank Steve and Dave for making it all happen. (I mean it's only been 35 years).

SPANISH TORTILLA

6 eggs, beaten

2 Yukon Gold potatoes

2 or 3 green onions, chopped until
light green parts

1/4 cup olive oil

Salt and fresh ground black pepper

Slice potatoes into 1/8 inch discs. Pour olive oil into a nine-inch cast iron skillet. (Must be able to put under oven broiler). Heat it over medium high until a test end piece of potato sizzles when it hit's the oil. Work potato slices in batches, frying one layer at a time until lightly browned. Dry on paper towels and salt and pepper to taste. Drain most of the olive oil. Sautee the onions until just crisp. Turn off pan. Spread onions evenly around the bottom of the pan. Top with potato slices in a scalloped pattern. Turn heat back to medium. Add eggs along with salt and pepper to taste. Shake the pan so eggs completely cover potatoes. Cook until the edges begin to set. Cook under broiler for 5 minutes until top is browned. Remove pan. Let cool for 5 minutes. Place a plate on top and invert pan. Remove pan and you have a Spanish Tortilla. Cut into wedges. This can be served cold as well, which how I had it in Zaragoza.

SHRIMP AND CHORIZO TAPAS

5 Tbl olive oil

2 tsp salt

1 lb chorizo

1 tsp black pepper

1 1/2 cups thinly sliced
onion

1 1/2 lbs peeled raw med
shrimp

2 cloves garlic, minced

3 tbl lemon juice

1/2 cup dry sherry

2 tbl minced parsley

1 tbl paprika

1 crusty baguette

Slice chorizo into ½ inch diagonals. Brown in one tbl olive for 7-8 minutes. Add onion, stirring off and on until caramelized, 4-6 minutes. Add garlic and ¼ cup sherry and stir for 1 minute. Devein shrimp. Add along with paprika, 1 tsp salt, ½ tsp black pepper and cook until pink, 4-5 minutes. Add remaining ingredients, stir to combine, and remove from heat. Spoon on small plates with juices and pass the bread for mopping up.

SUMMER SALAD SERENADE

Inspired Magazine Summer 2012

My wife, Brenda, is, without a doubt, the ultimate salad queen. Seriously, she would be satisfied and satiated if that was all she consumed for the rest of her life. Now, I'm not talking about chicken salad or tuna salad here. Nor that squiggly Jell-O thing with banana slices that always has a place at the family reunion. And what the h--- is that white puffy stuff with chocolate sprinkles on it? No, we're talking about food with a base of greens and a combination of fruits and vegetables and possibly a protein or two. When we go out to eat, I peruse the entire menu while Brenda teeters between an iceberg lettuce wedge with bleu cheese dressing and fresh bacon crumbles or the house Caesar salad with homemade croutons. I ask her if she wants to split an order of barbeque ribs or try the shrimp po'boy but she only has eyes for the salad section. Lets face it, when it comes to dining out, Brenda's bunny side hops forth.

Not that there's anything wrong with salads! They're very versatile. One of the finest tales on that subject is the creation of the Caesar salad. I've heard several different versions. The best embellishment is that two immigrant Italian brothers relocated in San Diego in the early 1900s. They opened a bar and restaurant in

Tijuana in order to circumvent the Prohibition laws. A lot of Hollywood celebrities would come down on weekends to legally party hearty. On one particular Sunday, the fourth of July, 1924, it was raining heavily, the streets were mud, and the Hollywood celebrities were literally stuck in town, hung over, and hungry. The restaurant had been crazy busy over the weekend, so Caesar Cardini, the brother on duty at the time, scrambled to put something together as they were almost out of everything. A little romaine lettuce, garlic, olive oil, lemon juice, Worcestershire sauce tossed with croutons and Parmesan cheese and Dwella!! Caesar salad is born. Probably the most famous salad coming out of the America's in the 20th century.

This is not an unusual occurrence in a restaurant kitchen. Actually, it probably happens a lot. Even in our kitchen. Recently Izac, our head chef, had a large amount of salmon filets left over from the weekend on Sunday morning. He pulled me aside and said "I'm thinking about pan searing these babies and serving it over some sort of salad." Fine. Next time I'm back in the kitchen I find him copiously studying cookbooks. (I always encourage my crew to copiously study.) An hour later he emerges with his dish. Unbelievable! He didn't create a salad; he created a magnificent piece of art! And the beauty of it all was everything he used were ingredients we have in our kitchen inventory. I went out and talked to the first person who ordered it. He said he was so enthralled enjoying it that he had not spoken a word to his companion for five minutes. Later, he told his waitperson that it was absolutely orgasmic.

So the point of all this is creativity, creativity, creativity! And if you absolutely want to astound your friends or say, your significant other, there is no better time than right now. Since we're highlighting the farmers markets this Inspire(d), I thought it would be appropriate to end up there – plus it's the perfect place to create a salad. The farmers markets are in full swing and it's a damn shame if you are missing out getting to one. I like to arrive early when the bursting cornucopia of the week's harvest is at its height. Usually, I don't go with an idea of what I want, so I like to do a full circuit of all of the booths, see what's to be had, and then thinking through, put together maybe a salad, a side, soup, or possibly even a main entree. Almost always, I will come across a new lettuce, vegetable, or fruit. The vendors and the customers are all yakking it up with each other, and invariably, they'll start telling me how they prepare this particular item or what they've paired it with. You know, like kumquats with fois gras or pan-seared dandelions with hard-boiled quail eggs. All kidding aside, there is a treasure trove of information to be mined at the farmers market (see page 78 for more tips on getting the most out of your Farmers Market). And besides, mingling with the diverse group there can be a great deal of fun. So start gathering up your favorites ingredients and let your bunny side shine.

Don't worry if you don't have every ingredient. Improvise. That's what this article is about. After all, you may be serving the best salad to come out of the 21st century!

EASY CAESAR SALAD

(serves 4 salad courses)

1 tsp kosher or sea salt

6 canned anchovy filets

2 garlic cloves crushed (patted dry
and minced)

4 T extra virgin olive oil

1 Large egg coddled*

2 T fresh lemon juice

1 head Romaine lettuce

2 T red wine vinegar

1/2 C fresh Parmesan cheese

1tsp Dijon mustard

1 tsp freshly ground black pepper

1 tsp Worcestershire sauce

2 cups croutons, homemade or store
bought

In a small mixing bowl add salt and garlic. Use a fork and mash garlic into salt. Make it
pretty small. Add olive oil, vinegar, mustard, Worcestershire sauce, anchovies, and egg.
Whisk vigorously and set aside. Trim lettuce, removing stem and top leaves. Chop into one-
inch pieces. Toss with dressing mixture. In a large bowl, top with Parmesan cheese, black
pepper, and croutons. Pass around and be delighted.

IZAC'S SALMON SALAD

(serves 4-main meal)

Salad Ingredients
16-20oz. Mixed greens

1 green pepper, halved and sliced
8 oz. cherry tomatoes, halved

8 oz Feta cheese
1 med red onion, sliced thin

2 oranges, 6 slices per
1 small cucumber, halved

2 lemons, 6 slices per
3 limes, 4 slices per sliced
lengthways

4 - 4 oz Salmon filets

4 T extra virgin olive oil

Marinade
Peel of one orange, diced
(Save orange interior)

1 C orange juice

Juice of one lemon

Salt and black pepper to taste

Glaze
Saved orange interior, diced

1/2 C orange juice

2 T honey

Salt black pepper to taste

Lemon Dressing
1/2 C extra virgin olive oil

1/4 C lemon juice

1 garlic clove, minced

Salt and black pepper to taste

Whisk all marinade ingredients together. In a small baking dish.(preferably glass, no aluminum) place salmon filets and cover with marinade. Refrigerate for one hour, turning once after 30 minutes. While salmon is marinating, combine glaze ingredients in a small pot and reduce over low -med heat on the stove until somewhat thickened. Set aside.

Now, lets build a salad. Mound lettuce on 4 dinner plates or large salad bowls. On at a time divide tomatoes, onion, cucumbers, and green peppers on each salad. Try a mound on each. (See picture). Divide lemon dressing equally on each. Add feta cheese to each. To each salad overlay on three sides, a slice each of orange, lemon, and lime. Set aside. Remove salmon from marinade and pat dry. Pan sear in extra virgin olive oil for 3 minutes over medium high heat. Turn over and brush with glaze mixture. Heat for another 2- 3 minutes depending on doneness wanted. A one-inch filet at 5 minutes total will probably get you to medium rare plus. Enjoy and tell Izac thanks the next time you see him.

AN ODE TO PIE

Inspired Magazine Fall 2012

O z never did give nothing to the Tin Man...
er... Pie Man... scratch that – in this case,
Pie Maven. As you may have surmised, this
column is dedicated to an exploration of eating
humble pie. And since creating scrumptious
pie isn't one of my strong suits, I decided to do
just that, and enlist the aid of the premier pie
maker I know, Julie Noel. Julie is our pastry
chef extraordinaire at the Dolce Vita. When
you walk into our kitchen and Julie is whipping
up an intoxicating concoction, the smells will

make you think you've died and are at the
pearly gates. Cheesecakes that are lighter than
air, mouthwatering fruit crisps, humongous
cookies, tantalizing kolaches, and the freshest
cinnamon rolls are just a few in her far-reaching
repertoire. But making pie is her finest forte.

So we talked pie. Julie immediately shared her
earliest recollection of the delightful pastry: She
was seven or eight and had walked home from
school to find a lemon pie on the counter. Her
aunt, also a great baker, made it for Julie. It was

a special treat because her mother made nothing from scratch, and the memory had Julie almost drooling. You know, she was living the pie life.

Julie has had no formal training as a pastry chef. She learned "by the seat of her pants and the school of hard knocks", and got her start making pies while working for Vesterheim at the Dayton House Café. It has been a love affair ever since. It is not unusual to find her making 25 to 30 pies for a wedding or an event.

So then we got to the *making* pie talk. This time of year there is always an abundance of fruit available so we concentrated on pies made with fresh apples, peaches, berries, and so on. Julie explained that the most important part of making pie is the crust. (Dough recipe to follow.) The dough consists of five basic ingredients: flour (preferably pastry flour), chilled fat, ice-cold water, sugar, and salt. Her most preferred fat is lard. All right!! Pork fat!! I'm loving it. For sweet

pies like we are concentrating on, you will want to use lard without any smoke flavor. Smoke flavored lards are great for savory pies such as quiche or chicken potpie. See, I learn something new every day. Thanks, Julie! If lard is not in your larder, then a combination of half butter and half Crisco is acceptable. Julie adds the dry ingredients together and then works the fat into the flour by hand. Water is added sparingly just to slightly moisten the dough as it is worked. She can make the perfect dough in her sleep. All the rest of us mere mortals probably are going to do a lot of dough 101 practice.

Being the dedicated researchers we are, Julie and I decided that a pie foray was in order. All right!! Road trip!! We deliberated long and hard as to where to satiate our pie appetites. Oh, for maybe three minutes. The Aroma Pie Shop in Whalen, Minnesota, beckoned us. Our intrepid group of pie seekers consisted of myself, my always fashionable wife, Brenda, Julie the Pie Maven, Fawn (daughter and other baker), and two precocious and potential pie professionals, August (eight) and Stella (two and a half) (grandchildren). We stopped in Lanesboro for lunch at the Riverside on the Root. After burgers and salads and three trips up to the trestle bridge on the bike trail crossing the Root River, we walked up town to The Spud Boy Diner, the only wood wheeled diner left in the United States. Gordon and Val Tindall operate it seven days a week from April through October with inside seating for 20 and a kitchen area so small you have to step outside to change your mind. Gordon was sitting outside and asked me what we were doing in town. I explained our pie mission. Immediately he informed me that he had made a blueberry and peach pie that very morning. OK! I nabbed a slice and had it for breakfast the next morning. Delicious. Both fruits complemented each other perfectly.

The women in the group decided they would like to shop for a while, so August and I headed to the bike store to buy some fishing bait. August had brought along his pole in case the opportunity to drop a line arose. We proceeded to the city park where there are two trout stocked ponds. Nothing was biting on spinners so worm drowning was in order for the next hour. When the rest of our party returned, it was time to fly for pie.

A few minutes down the road, we pulled in front of the Aroma Pie Shop. I parked in the shade under a big maple tree because one of our potential pie professionals (Stella) had slipped off into slumber land. I'm sure she was dreaming of a big slice of pie and eating with her fingers and smearing it across her face. I know my granddaughter. Fawn stayed in the van with her and the rest of us proceeded into the pie shop.

And there was pie to behold. I think they had 16 different types ranging from fruits to banana cream to key lime. I spoke with the owner, Maggie Gerges. She says she has three fulltime bakers. They bake the pies fresh every day. On real busy days they have baked up to 100 pies. All of the crusts are made with lard. (There's that pork fat thing again.) And they're scrumptious. I had a piece of blackberry, Brenda strawberry rhubarb, Julie peach, and August banana cream with two scoops of ice cream and a root beer float. What can I say, he's a growing boy. Julie's first pie-expert reaction was "This is just perfect. The crust is terrific and the natural flavor of the fruit comes out. Sugar has not been added in proportions to overpower the real fruit taste." I agreed.

Ah yes, pie. A wonderful experience. I'd recommend it to anyone. I mean… all we are saying is give a piece a chance!

JULIE'S APPLE PIE

Crust:

2 1/4 cups flour

1/4 cup sugar

1/2 tsp salt

1/4 cup Crisco chilled

1/3 cup butter chilled

1/3 to ½ cup ice water

Filling:

3 Granny Smith apples

4 Golden Delicious apples

2/3 cup sugar

1/2 cup flour

1/2 tsp cinnamon

2 Tbl butter

Glaze:

2 Tbl Cream

1 egg white

Sugar

By hand, mix all crust ingredients except ice water in a mixing bowl. Add by sprinkles water as needed to form a ball. Divide in half. Press into two circles and roll into two twelve inch circles. This is best done on a cool surface. Place one crust in the bottom of a 10-inch deep-dish pie pan. Overlap the edge and trim off excess. Mix all filling ingredients and put in pie pan. Cut butter into 8 pieces and dot ingredients. Cover with remaining crust. Trim excess. Crimp edges with a fork. Whisk cream and egg white. Brush top of pie. Make 3 slits on top of pie. Sprinkle with sugar. Bake at 375 degrees 50-60 minutes until golden brown and filling is bubbling.

A CHICKEN IN EVERY POT

...OR THE MAGICAL POWERS OF CHICKEN NOODLE SOUP

Inspired Magazine Winter 2012

Which came first the chicken or the egg? Honestly? Who cares. Both are delightful ingredients for a winter/cold/flu season staple: chicken (egg) noodle soup!

Chicken noodle is not just any soup. It's a soup that is cherished by many cultures throughout the world. Many different versions abound. Today ours is made from scratch with handmade egg noodles. Oh yeah baby, not your mama's Campbell's Soup, that's for sure.

So lets get started. Broth is the key ingredient. You can use canned or boxed chicken broth. NOT!! (Well, maybe in a pinch, I guess. NOT!!!) Using a homemade broth in soups is just so far superior to the store-bought versions. There are a couple of ways I make my own broth (and you can too!). At the restaurant, we bake a lot of chicken. And, consequently, we have a lot of pan juices that we save. Think of it as liquid gold. We let the juices cool, and skim off any fat that might rise. The juices are then poured into plastic containers with tight lids. These we date using freezer tape and store in our freezer for future use. We pull out as needed, oldest first. Since we are constantly using the juices for soups and gravies, we don't have to worry about shelf life, but if you're not breaking out the big pots as often as us, a year is the max to store and I personally would toss after six months. When ready to use, thaw your stock-base out in the refrigerator the previous day. This base is naturally concentrated, so all you have to do is add water and seasonings (salt, pepper, herbs to taste) to fill out your soup. This works well if you have leftover chicken that you'd like to toss into a soup.

Another great way to make broth is to take a whole plucked and thawed chicken, remove the liver and any excess fat, and put it, along with about three to four inches of water, in a large pot. Bring to a boil, reduce to a simmer, and cover. Cook for about an hour. Usually, when the chicken floats, you are good to go. To make sure, use tongs and grab a leg. If it becomes detached, chicken is ready to go. If not, simmer a few minutes longer. Remove the chicken and let broth cool. Skim off the fat and it's time to make soup, with your chicken AND stock ready to go.

Congratulations! You have just passed Chicken Broth 101!

Let's move on to handmade egg noodles. Every good egg noodle has a story behind it. Mine goes like this: I was living in Iowa City in the early 1970s. Every few weeks I would come back to Decorah for the weekend. I have some great friends, Steve Olson (Ole) and Juanita Riveria (Goochie). They were living up by Burr Oak, it was winter, and I arrived at the door. "Come on in." I walked into the kitchen and here was Goochie covered with flour, rolling out dough that almost completely covered the four by six-foot wooden kitchen table. "What's going on,

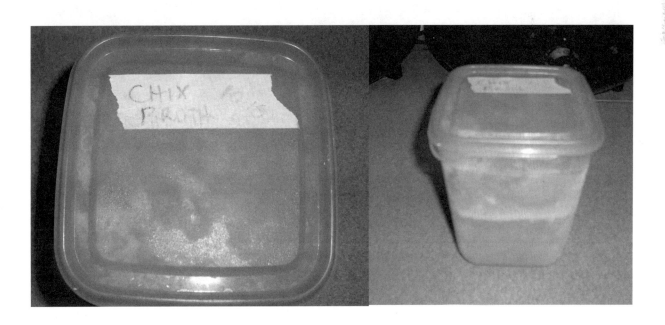

Goochie?" I queried. "Well, Barb Winter gave me a couple of chickens and I'm going to make chicken noodle soup. But first I have to make noodles and you can help." I reply, "Ok, I'm in, but I've never done this before." Fortunately, for Goochies sake, I am a quick learner and soon we were slicing the dough into long noodles and draping them onto any available space to dry. Backs of chairs, hung over counters, off of the table, etc. Man, noodle art at its finest. It would have made Andy Warhol proud. Thanks for the lesson, Goochie! If you have never had fresh-made egg noodles you are in for one of life's great treats. I guarantee it is bliss.

After all that noodling, it's time to really sweat. Veggies that is. Like your mother always said, eat your vegetables! I like to sauté the veggies that I put in my soups. When they start to get soft, they also start to lose their water. I find this accentuates the vegetable flavors. The unami of soup flavor. Add it all to the pot. Yummy, to say the least. Of course we still have to have seasoning. The key word here is fresh. Just remember fresh is best when it comes to herbs. In almost all of my soups I like to use fresh thyme. It is extremely versatile. Then I crank it up with additional herbs. Sage really works well with poultry related dishes. My mom was a big

fan of sage. Although she primarily used dried herbs, she always said sage should be a big part of poultry dishes. And I always listened to my mom. You should too. Your mom, I mean, not mine. So into the chicken soup the fresh sage goes.

Now that your chicken soup is seasoned, put it to use for another season: the holiday season. It's all about sharing with your loved ones and friends, and a great way to start off this giving time of year is to divvy up a steaming hot bowl of chicken soup for everyone. Pass around some crusty bread and pour a crispy white wine. Enjoy the camaraderie and spread the love. This also works for the cold/flu season as you share the healing powers of chicken soup. It's truly a magical winter concoction.

CHICKEN NOODLE SOUP

1 3 1/2 -4 lb. whole chicken
Water
1/3 cup olive oil
6 stalks celery, chopped
4 large carrots, peeled and
   chopped
1 large onion, diced

4 cloves garlic, minced
Homemade egg noodles (recipe to follow)
1/4 cup fresh lemon juice
2 sprigs fresh thyme, minced
1 Tbl fresh sage, minced
Salt and fresh ground black pepper to taste

Remove liver and excess fat from chicken. Place in a large pot and cover with water by 3-4 inches. Bring to a boil and reduce to a simmer for about an hour. Meanwhile, pour olive oil in a large skillet. Sauté celery and carrots over medium heat for 3 minutes. Add onions and garlic and sauté 3 minutes more. When chicken is thoroughly cooked (see column directions) pull from broth and let cool. Let broth cool somewhat and skim broth off.

When chicken is sufficiently cooled remove skin. Remove meat from bones and dice. Bring broth back to a simmer. Add sautéed vegetables and noodles. Add lemon juice and spices, adjusting as needed. Soup is good to go when noodles are nice and chewy.

HOMEMADE NOODLES

1 1/2 cups flour
2 eggs

2 teaspoons salt
Water

Make a mound of flour on your work surface. Make a well in the center. Whisk eggs and salt. Place in well. Slowly, by hand, mix flour and egg mixture until eggs are incorporated. If the mixture is to dry, add water a little at a time until you have a pliable ball of dough. Cover and let rest for 10 minutes. Divide in half. Roll out each half as thin as possible. Take a sharp paring knife and cut into strips, however wide you want your noodles to be. Hang off of counters and chair backs to dry, about an hour.